Choose Life And Not Death

Choose Life And Not Death
(A Primer on Abortion, Euthanasia and Suicide)

By

Rev. William F. Maestri

ALBA · HOUSE   NEW · YORK

SOCIETY OF ST. PAUL, 2187 VICTORY BLVD., STATEN ISLAND, NEW YORK 10314

Library of Congress Cataloging in Publication Data

Maestri, William.
    Choose life and not death.

    Bibliography: p.
    1. Abortion—Moral and ethical aspects. 2. Euthana-
sia—Moral and ethical aspects. 3. Suicide—Moral and
ethical aspects. 4. Christian ethics. I. Title.
RG734.M34   1986   174'.24   85-28687
ISBN 0-8189-0490-9

Nihil Obstat:
John H. Miller, C.S.C., S.T.D.
Censor Librorum

Imprimatur:
† Most Rev. Philip M. Hannan
November 27, 1985

The Nihil Obstat and Imprimatur are
a declaration that a book or pamphlet is considered
to be free from doctrinal or moral error. It is not implied
that those who have granted the Nihil Obstat and
Imprimatur agree with the contents,
opinions or statements expressed.

Designed, printed and bound in the United States of
America by the Fathers and Brothers of the
Society of St. Paul, 2187 Victory Boulevard,
Staten Island, New York 10314, as part of their
communications apostolate.

1 2 3 4 5 6 7 8 9 (Current Printing: first digit)

Contents

Introduction

The title of this book comes from the thirtieth chapter of the book of Deuteronomy. Verses fifteen through twenty capture a moment of high drama and decision-making for the people of Israel. The people have reached a crossroads of tremendous importance. Set before them are the two ways of existing: one is the way of obedience and love for the Lord and His covenant. This way produces life. Then there is the way of disobedience and pride. Such a way leads to death.

Moses makes clear what is at stake. "If you obey the commandments of the Lord your God which I command this day, by loving the Lord your God, by walking in his ways, and by keeping his commandments and statutes and ordinances, then you shall live and multiply, and the Lord your God will bless you in the land which you are entering to take possession of it." By contrast, "if your heart turns away, and you will not hear, but are drawn away to worship other gods and serve them, I declare to you this day, that you shall perish; you shall not live long in the land which you are going over the Jordan to enter and possess."

There is no middle ground. The nation must decide whether it will choose life or death. The moral leadership of Moses is clear: ". . . choose life, that you and your descendants may live, loving the Lord your God, obeying his voice, and cleaving to him; for that means life to you and length of days, that you may dwell in the land which the Lord swore to your fathers, to Abraham, to Isaac, and to Jacob, to give them."

This dramatic scene in Deuteronomy, the choices facing Israel, and the moral leadership of Moses are more than interesting episodes in our religious past. They powerfully confront us today. In many ways we stand in the same position as Israel in the wilderness. We face some of the most challenging and agonizing issues of life and death. We are in desperate need of moral leadership. The decisions we make will affect not only the present but those who will come after us (at least those whom we *permit* to come after us!).

There are five (5) major themes in these six verses which demand our attention and offer valuable guidance as we struggle to choose life.

The *first* major theme is the experience of *wilderness*. Israel finds herself in a new situation in which the old landmarks no longer have the power to guide. The people have gone from slavery to freedom. The oppression of Egyptian masters has been replaced by the covenant of Yahweh. This new relationship requires new thinking and the responsibility of making hard choices. Today our less than brave new world of bio-medical technologies has ushered us into a wilderness where the old landmarks have been swept aside. The power of these technologies and the miracles of modern medicine have extended life and enhanced the quality of that life. However, none of these advances have come free of charge. New advances in biology and medicine have raised some of the most perplexing problems facing humankind.

Among the many issues we now face in this new situation, the following are crucial: What does it mean to be a person? What is the value of human life? When does human life begin? How are we to treat the human being at the "edges of life"? What are the criteria for death? Can we morally take our life when it is too much of a burden? Can we take the life of another who no longer desires to live?

These questions, and many more, are the moral choices that

now lay before us. As Israel could not turn back to Egypt (although the temptation was great and advocated by some), modern man cannot uninvent the technology which has brought us to our own crossroads in the wilderness.

The *second* major theme or parallel is the need for *moral guidance*. The issues we confront today—abortion, euthanasia, and suicide—touch the deepest chords of our personal and collective moral identities. Hence they are bound to evoke the deepest feelings. Unfortunately, intensity of feeling does not necessarily lead to clarity of thought or loving behavior. As we know only too well, there has been much heat but little moral light. Slogans fill the air. Charges and counter-charges make dialogue impossible. We find ourselves in a "dialogue of the deaf" in which we shout about or at one another rather than speak with and to one another. We can easily find ourselves being fiercely committed to life issues but all the while lacking the love of Jesus for others (even those with whom we disagree).

The religious and moral leadership we need is much like that exhibited by Moses. Moses refrains from shouting, threatening, and becoming just another shrill voice. He calls the people together and presents the options. Moses trusts the community to respond in a way that is loving of God and respectful of life. Israel is at the crossroads and the decisions to be made are no small matter. Moses does not pretend to be a neutral observer *simply* laying out the options and then following the will of the majority. He is a leader who is committed yet respectful of the community. Moses clearly indicates he wants the people to choose life and the covenant with the Lord.

However, there is always the chance that freedom will be abused and the commuity will follow idols. Authentic moral leadership must constantly wrestle with the tension of *trusting* the community to follow the Spirit and walk in the Lord. The renowned bio-ethicist Richard A. McCormick, S.J. writes:

True leadership calls forth the best in those led. It liberates them into the fullness of their potential and most generally by moving minds and hearts. Jesus' love is the paradigm here. It is effective. It empowers us, makes us "new creatures."   (*Health and Medicine In the Catholic Tradition*)

The *third* major theme concerns the *social morality* of the three issues that we shall examine in this book. The covenant between God and Israel is a social reality and requires the knowledge and commitment of all the people. The decisions facing Israel were ones in which each person had a stake in the outcome. Today much of the social dimensions of life, especially the moral dimensions, are obscured behind a veil of radical individualism and individual rights. The great issues of the day are not debated in the public square which is now naked (Richard Neuhaus). Rather, political issues are decided in terms of self-interest and moral issues are settled on the basis of private choice (John Noonan, Jr.).

For example, abortion (one could easily add euthanasia and suicide) is removed from public debate and moral claims because it is deemed "a woman's right to do with her body as she pleases. This choice to abort or not to abort is hers alone. Neither society, father, nor the child in the womb have any rights claims. Abortion is exclusively a woman's issue."

Dr. Daniel Callahan, Ph.D. is the Director of the Hastings Center and holds a somewhat liberal view of abortion. However, he rejects as myth the belief that abortion is an issue to be decided only by a woman. Dr. Callahan makes three telling points.

First, even though he does not want male approval to be written into the law, he believes "there is an injustice in giving males no rights prior to birth but then imposing upon them a full range of obligations after birth."

Secondly, the belief that child-bearing and rearing are simply matters of private choice is a blatant disregard for social consequences. Callahan writes, "To imply that woman alone should have all the rights, even though the consequences involve the lives of both sexes, is an unfair conclusion . . . child-bearing and child-rearing have consequences for everyone in society."

And finally, it must be admitted that an unborn child is *in* the woman's body, however, not in the same way as an arm or a leg is *part* of one's body. Dr. Callahan writes, "The separate genetic constitution of the fetus, its rate of growth and development, and its separate organ system clearly distinguish the body of the fetus from the body of the mother" ("Abortion: Some Ethical Issues," Daniel Callahan, *Abortion, Society and the Law*).

A retreat from the social into the highly privatized world of individual rights and liberties was one of the major driving forces behind the Supreme Court decision of Roe v. Wade. The Supreme Court declared that each act of abortion is a highly private choice to be made by the woman alone. The noted philosopher and legal scholar John T. Noonan, Jr. writes:

> Each act of abortion is, by declaration of the Supreme Court of the United States, a private decision. Yet each act of abortion bears on the structure of marriage and the family, the role and duties of parents, the limitations of the paternal part in procreation, and the virtues that characterize a mother. Each act of abortion bears on the orientation and responsibilities of the obstetrician, the nurse, the hospital administrator, and the hospital trustee. The acceptance of abortion affects the professor and student of medicine and the professor and student of law. In the United States, abortion on a large scale requires the participation of the federal and state governments. Overarching the whole system of private choice is the command of the judiciary. (*A Private Choice*)

Simply put: there is very little that is private about the so-called private choice of abortion. Abortion concerns more than the woman. Society as a whole is involved.

Moses reminds the people of their past and their future in helping them to make a wise decision. If they choose the covenant with the Lord and life, they are paying honor to the memory of their ancestors and laying the groundwork for life for those who come after. Actions done in the present grow out of past tradition, and will help to shape the future. Hence, the *fourth* theme concerns a respect for our *moral tradition* and a deep concern for *future generations*.

The issues of abortion, euthanasia and suicide touch on a fundamental value of human existence and society—*life*. The way in which we value life grows out of our past traditions and becomes the legacy we leave to those whose past we wait to become. The moral issues of today's bio-medical world are complex. Yet this does not mean we cannot look to our past for guidance and insight. This is especially true of the Catholic moral tradition. Bio-ethicist Thomas A. Shannon writes, "One tradition in Roman Catholic moral theology, especially in America, has been the development of a set of ethical teachings related specifically to medicine. While much of this grew out of a genuine sense of pastoral concern for both the patient and physician, there was also a theoretical probing of the issues themselves." ("The Tradition of a Tradition: An Evaluation of Roman Catholic Medical Ethics").

Throughout our study we hope to befriend our biblical faith and the Catholic moral tradition. We hope to be like the wise servant, commended by Jesus, who was able to draw new insights from the treasury of his tradition.

Moses indicated that the people not only choose life for themselves but, in choosing the covenant relationship with the Lord, they are also laying a claim for the future. The way in which we value the unborn indicates the degree to which we are willing to protect life that is voiceless and vulnerable. Our respect for the dying reveals the extent to which we continue to care even when the powers of curing have ceased. And the legal and political climate we create goes a long way in witnessing the depth of our commitment to life and all that enhances this precious gift. Those who come after us will inherit what we do today. On the day of judgment they will rise to bless us or condemn us.

The *fifth* and final theme concerns the *story of God* (John Shea) which structures our community life and plays a normative role in the formation of character. One of the more important tasks of a community is the building of moral identity and character. The tools that go into such moral formation are more than rules, principles and laws. Underlying our ethics and morals is a story (us) about the good, actions that befit human beings, and the goals that the just society ought to achieve or at least strive for. For the Christian community there is something even more foundational. At its center is the story or narrative of God. Christian character formation occurs within a community that is guided by the stories of God. These stories shape the community, and the community helps to shape and apply them to contemporary issues.

Ethicist Stanley Hauerwas has done some of the most creative work in ethics using the narrative or story character of community life. He writes:

> The nature of Christian ethics is determined by the fact that Christian convictions take the form of a story, or perhaps better, a set of stories that constitutes a tradition, which in turn creates and forms a community. Christian ethics does not begin by emphasizing rules or principles, by calling our attention to a narrative that tells of God's dealing with creation . . . There is no more fundamental way to talk of God than in a story. The fact that we come to

know God through the recounting of the story of Israel and
the life of Jesus is decisive for our truthful understanding of
the kind of God we worship as well as the world in which
we exist.   (*The Peaceable Kingdom*)

The Christian community's stories of God hold that He is the
author and giver of all life. God gives life out of love and loves us
into eternity. He wants us to be with Him in the Kingdom
forever. Professor Hauerwas reminds us that the stories of God
we tell center on two crucial insights: ". . . we know ourselves
truthfully only when we know ourselves in relation to God. We
know who we are only when we can place ourselves—locate our
stories—within God's story . . . For our God is a God who wills
to include us within his life." And the second crucial insight
concerns the way we understand human life: "To learn to be
God's creature, to accept the gift, is to learn to be at home in
God's world."

The Christian community is formed both by a very specific
story (us) of God, and by the person of Jesus. Again Hauerwas
writes, "To be a Christian implies substantive and profound
convictions about the person and work of Jesus of Nazareth . . .
the Gospel is the story of a man who had the authority to preach
that the Kingdom of God is present." The story of the Kingdom
is one in which a community and character is formed so that we
can learn "to live without fear of one another" (cf. *A Community
of Character*, by Stanley Hauerwas. Of special interest is chapter
2: "Jesus: The Story of the Kingdom").

The stories of God, the profound convictions we hold about
the normative character of Jesus and the Kingdom, and the
resulting view of human life have crucial implications for the
issues of abortion, euthanasia and suicide. These life issues rest
on how we value life and the limits to fostering and preserving
human life. In the final analysis life issues raise the following
question: Is human life a gift from a loving God who wants to

share His life with us? Or, is human life a possession to be used and disposed of as we see fit? Life, its enhancement and termination, raises some of the most profound questions about our relationship with God and one another.

The scope of this book is limited. We shall examine three (3) major moral issues that have forced us to rethink our deepest held convictions about life—abortion, euthanasia and suicide. This book is a primer or introduction, and hence we do not pretend to tell the reader "everything he or she might want to know about these life issues." Our goal is more modest. We hope to introduce the reader to these issues in light of the modern medical-moral situation. We also want to examine these highly complex and often emotional issues in light of our biblical faith and the Catholic moral tradition. Therefore, we do not pretend to approach our subjects from a value-free stance.

The author is a Catholic priest who lives, moves and has his being firmly within a community of faith. This faith, and the stories that have helped nurture that faith, will influence what follows. Rather than considering this a liability, we consider it a great gain. There is no pretense that what follows is simply a laying out of options. Like Moses, the author does not engage in ethical reflection without a qualifier. These reflections grow out of the Catholic-Christian community.

Our inquiry will open with a discussion of the meaning of *bio-medical ethics*. We shall then turn our attention to the rich insights of the Roman Catholic tradition in the field of medical ethics. From this moral tradition there emerges a number of principles that have become crucial for the determination of bio-medical ethics. This first chapter will conclude with the biblical perspective on the value of human life and its relationship to God.

Chapter Two will introduce us to the most controversial and emotional issue facing us as a society, namely abortion. We will briefly review the definition of abortion and the various types of abortions performed. Then we shall turn our attention to the legal developments that have taken place since the landmark Supreme Court decision of *Roe v. Wade* (1973). Of crucial importance will be the necessity of distinguishing the legal and the moral. All that is legal is not necessarily moral. Abortion is more than a political and legal issue. It is a profoundly moral issue. Hence, we want to examine the abortion issue in light of our biblical faith and the Catholic moral tradition. Finally, we shall bring this chapter to a close with a pastoral approach to those who are considering abortion and to those who have already had an abortion.

Chapter Three raises the troubling issue of euthanasia. Once again we will befriend our biblical and Catholic traditions concerning the sacredness of life, and then explore the meaning of euthanasia with its various distinctions. Our attention will then turn to the complex legal situation on euthanasia. Euthanasia invites us to reflect on some of the deepest aspects of our spirituality concerning illness, suffering and death. We must do more than merely speak for life; we must actively care for each person, especially the sick and dying. Therefore, our discussion of euthanasia will end with a reflection on pastoral care to the sick and dying.

Chapter Four will examine the last of our life issues—suicide. More and more today we hear the expressions, "the right to die" and "rational suicide" being voiced in our society. We will want to examine the meaning of these expressions and contrast them with the Christian understanding of life as gift and each person as a steward of that gift. Special attention will be paid to the *Declaration on Euthanasia* by the Sacred Congregation. Our discussion will close with a pastoral reflection on ministry to those who have attempted or are considering suicide.

Chapter Five will attempt to review and synthesize our discussions on the three life issues (abortion, euthanasia and suicide). Yet this is not a mere summary; we will present a vision of what it means to live life in abundance as individuals and as a people. At the center of this vision is the Person of Jesus Christ. It is His story, and the stories He tells about the Kingdom and His Father, that structure Christian community life and form character. We shall close our study of these life issues with a reaffirmation of the pastoral ministry of the Church on behalf of life as God's gift.

At the end of this volume we have included the following: a *series of cases* dealing with the life-issues discussed, along with some questions for discussion. Appendix I contains the text of the excellent statement by the Vatican Congregation for the Doctrine of the Faith on Euthanasia published in 1980. Appendix II contains the text of a talk given by Joseph Cardinal Bernardin entitled, "Consistent Ethic of Life." This talk was delivered on June 7, 1984 at the National Right to Life Convention in Kansas City, Missouri. Many of the pro-life themes earlier articulated by Cardinal Bernardin (at Fordham and St. Louis University) are contained and developed in this address. Finally, we have included an extensive bibliography and resource section which can aid the reader to further study and reflection.

Before proceeding on to Chapter One gratitude and acknowledgment are in order. For a key ingredient in life is the realization of how much we owe to our fellows. The origin of this book belongs not to me but to Father Victor L. Viberti, SSP, former Provincial of the Society of St. Paul and currently acquisitions editor of ALBA HOUSE at Staten Island. While Father Viberti conceived the idea for this book, he in no way is responsible for its shortcomings and limitations.

Gratitude is expressed to the medical community at Charity Hospital which trained me in radiologic technology and allows me to teach medical ethics. I am appreciative of St. Joseph Seminary College and the Benedictine Monks of St. Joseph Abbey who have extended the warmest of hospitality in the spirit of St. Benedict. A special thanks is extended to Mercy Academy in New Orleans. It was in this Catholic girls' high school that I first taught courses in bio-medical ethics to an outstanding group of honors science students. I offer my sincere thanks to Wilbur Brown, Jr. who typed the manuscript, corrected my spelling, and helped generally to bring order out of chaos.

My deepest gratitude is extended to Elaine and Ferdinand Maestri whose "yes" to life has made this book, by this writer, possible in a most profound way.

William F. Maestri
St. Joseph Seminary College
St. Benedict, Louisiana

A PRIMER ON ABORTION, EUTHANASIA AND SUICIDE

I

What Is Bio-Medical Ethics?

Foundations

No matter how strong a building may appear, the wise man checks the foundation. No matter how appealing the used car on the lot appears, the prudent consumer knows there is no substitute for looking under the hood and kicking the tires. In this opening chapter we hope to check the foundation, look under the hood, and kick the tires of our ethical inquiries into abortion, euthanasia and suicide. For the reflections that follow rest on our deepest and most elementary values concerning life and the human person. We must submit our foundational stories, values and principles to reflection in order to more deeply appreciate and understand our commitments to life and the dignity of all persons.

First of all what do we mean by ethics? Andrew C. Varga, S.J. in his helpful little book, *On Being Human*, defines ethics as "the study of the rightness and wrongness of human actions." Ethics is a normative science based on rules, principles and norms by which we judge the correctness of human behavior. In other words, ethics is not merely descriptive but prescriptive. That is, ethics prescribes what is to be done and avoided if one is to live a moral, virtuous life. The norms, rules and virtues are based on our common, universal nature. Hence, the principles of ethics are not arbitrarily formulated but grow out of reflection on the meaning of being human. This reflection on what it means to be human and the behavior that befits humans is an ongoing, never ending task.

Having said that ethics is the reflection on the rightness and wrongness of human behavior based on a shared human nature, this can give one the impression that ethics is nothing but deducing principles for action. The moral life is reduced to nothing more than external, behavioral conformity to derived principles. Conformity becomes the highest virtue. While not wanting to deny the importance of principles (we shall be examining some key moral principles in bio-medical ethics) for the moral life, there is something greater than principles at work. The hope of ethical reflection and the goal of the moral life are to help form a virtuous character. The moral life is ultimately concerned about the kind of person (character) that is emerging through the acts one performs. Principles, values, rules and virtues are means to help form the moral character of a person and community. Principles are for the service of man; man does not exist for the service of our principles. William F. May, Professor of Ethics at Georgetown University, writes:

> Moralists make a mistake when they concentrate solely on the quandaries that practitioners face, or on the defects of the structures in which they operate. Inquiry into these matters already assumes specific dispositions of character, which themselves need to be classified and criticized . . . contemporary moralists have been much less interested than their predecessors in the clarification and cultivation of those virtues upon which the health of personal and social life depends.
>
> ("Professional Ethics: Setting, Terrain, and Teacher")

Professor May reminds us that ethics and the moral life are

much deeper than external conformity to principles and the solving of hard cases (a favorite activity in the field of bio-medical ethics). The moral life is fundamentally concerned with the moral identity of the person and the community (or profession).

In his outstanding book, *The Physician's Covenant*, Professor May further develops his understanding of ethics. Ethics is connective vision. By this he means that "ethics . . . has as its primary and direct intention not the bending of the will, the stirring of the feelings, or the manipulation of behavior, but the illumination of the understanding." It is directed to insight and vision. Ethics as corrective vision challenges the distorted social construction of reality that comes to us through science, the media, and our culture. Ethics challenges our taken-for-granted world of values and behavior. It forces us to constantly re-evaluate what we hold to be virtuous and good. Ethics fights the chains of ideology and rationalization which confirm us in our all too comfortable life style. Moral blindness is strong and seductive.

> The seductive feature of immoral behavior is that it always seems plausible. Although warped and distorted, the world so perceived makes its demands upon men and women . . . No one is so much the scoundrel that he does not think of his behavior as justified, as conforming to the world as it is. The man who hates believes that there are enemies out there to be hated . . . Immoral behavior is tempting because it seems the most reasonable response to the vision of the world which vice itself represents.
>
> (May, "Professional Ethics")

This notion of ethics as corrective vision is not an abandonment of reason; rather, it indicates that reason is vulnerable to distortion and manipulation. Ethics seeks to help reason "see" more clearly and hence allow reason to be open to the truth that sets us free. Again Professor May:

> Moral reflection attempts, at its best, a knowledgeable revisioning of the world that human practice presents. Corrective vision of this sort offers an immensely practical freedom. We cannot change our behavior unless, in some respects, our perception of the world also changes. In this task, the ethicist theorizes—quite literally—and thus helps liberate.   (*The Physician's Covenant*)

So far we have indicated that ethics and the moral life require a pattern of behavior that befits human beings and the formation of a character that is virtuous. We then indicated that this requires a vision that empowers us to make decisions which foster a virtuous character. We must now proceed one step further. There must be a content or story which corrects and interprets the way we live in the world as an individual and as a community. This statement needs to be qualified. That means we need to be specific about the tradition which forms our vision and character. As already mentioned, this book is informed by the Catholic Christian tradition.

Just what does the Christian story tell? How does this story influence our ethical reflections on life issues? The Christian story proclaims that God is the loving Giver of all life, and the Sanctifying Lover who transforms our hearts of stone to hearts of flesh. It proclaims that God is the God of life, who wants to share His life with us for eternity. Our life is not a possession to be controlled and manipulated; we must reverence it because we see in the goodness of life the goodness of Him who alone is good. The Christian story forms a community that lives in the freedom of the truth. We are truly God's sons and daughters. We need not live in fear and self-deception, trying to pretend that we are creators rather than creatures. Because life is a gift, none of us lives and dies as our own master. We belong to the Lord, and we shall know true peace and joy to the extent that we let God's story be told in our lives. We lay aside the will-to-power in order to let God's will be done in and through us. Sin is basically our drive to dominate and control—to live as if we are the captain of the ship. The great Protestant theologian Reinhold Niebuhr writes:

> Man is ignorant and involved in the limitations of a finite mind; but he pretends that he is not limited. He assumes that he can gradually transcend finite limitations until his mind becomes identical with universal mind. All of his intellectual and cultural pursuits, therefore, become infected with the sin of pride . . . The religious dimension of sin is man's rebellion against God, his effort to usurp the place of God. The moral and social dimension of sin is injustice. The ego which falsely makes itself the centre of existence in its pride and will and thus does injustice to other life.   (*The Nature and Destiny of Man*)

How does the Christian story influence our ethical reflections on the life issues of abortion, euthanasia and suicide? In each of these issues we witness around us a very materialistic view of the value assigned to human life. Namely, that life is a personal or individual possession to be disposed of by the owner of the body. Human life is seen as a property right to be disposed of as one sees fit. There is no transcendental dignity recognized in the human person. Life is not a gift but a possession to be used as one pleases. Likewise, human life is valued as long as it is desired, functioning, or meets the standards of acceptability by one's society. Hence, abortion is (mis)understood as a private choice by the woman alone. She is free to do what she wants with her body. The unborn child is a piece of property to be kept or discarded solely on the basis of the woman's free, private choice.

Euthanasia is the termination of one's life or that of another on the basis of whether or not one desires to live anymore. A life that is too burdensome to oneself (and in time to others), or one that does not possess a sufficient quality of life, or the capacity for relationships and reasoning no longer has a right to exist. The same can be said of suicide. Man understands himself as the master of his coming, staying and going. The direct termination of one's life is a rejection of the gift of life and fails to acknowledge the authorship of God. In all three of these instances we see clearly what Niebuhr wrote about: the illusion of omnipotence, the rebellion against God, the sin of pride, and the inevitable subordination and will-to-dominate others that does injustice to all of life.

Before we examine the distinctive features of bio-medical ethics let us briefly summarize our observations.

1. Individual human acts are morally important. An important, though, not exclusive, element of ethics is reflection on human acts as to their rightness and wrongness. There are human acts which befit and perfect human nature and there are acts which stunt our humanity.

2. Rules, principles, values and virtues are important for ethical reflection and the living of the moral life. However, these rules and principles are not ends in themselves but means or guidelines for the development of a moral character. The moral life is concerned about the deepest levels of moral identity, character, that is being formed by the acts we commit.

3. The development of character and the fostering of the moral life takes place in a community grounded in a given tradition (a qualifier). We have grounded our character formation in the Catholic Christian community. We tell, and are formed, by the stories of Israel and Jesus. God is the God of life and wants to share the Divine life with us. For our part we are called to reverence the gift of life and allow our personal story to be formed by God's story for all creation. Abortion, euthanasia

and suicide are direct challenges to God's authorship of life.

The Life Sciences and Human Values

A local television station in New Orleans devoted an entire week of special reports to the new advances in bio-medical technologies. The reporter, a most competent woman, interviewed physicians, lawyers, scientists and young couples about the various new reproductive technologies—*in vitro* fertilization, artificial insemination by husband (AIH) and by donor (AID), and some futuristic proposals concerning cloning, the artificial womb and cross-breeding between animals and humans. The entire week was informative and seductively satisfying except for one crucial element: there was not a word mentioned about ethics, values and the social consequences of these new reproductive technologies. These fascinating and troubling topics were treated in a way that gave the impression that no value issues were involved. The report was not immoral but amoral. As a postscript to the reports the news-anchor found much to support in these new technologies. He went further to indicate that anyone who chose to participate would do so on the basis of making "a very private choice."

These reports troubled me to the point of calling the station and speaking with the reporter. I expressed my concern over a lack of sensitivity to the ethical issues involved. The reporter was most receptive and promised to do a week of reports on the ethical concerns surrounding the new biology. True to her word she telephoned me and several others in order to produce a series on the values questions surrounding reproductive technologies. The reporter thanked me for my concern and for raising such issues. I relate this story not only to indicate that the media can be responsive to a listener's concerns, but also to indicate that often we are not sensitive to the moral dimension of life.

The lack of sensitivity to the moral dimensions of life is especially acute in the areas of science, medicine and technology. We often assume that these activites are value-free and simply concerned with facts and objective information. By contrast values are private, subjective and highly emotional. In other words, the world of science and the world of values have nothing in common and are best left to do their own thing. The mixing of science and values is destructive to both.

The above view, while quite common today, is unfortunate for both science and ethics. A valueless science becomes an end in itself, which leads to the dehumanization of *both* the scientist and the society at large. For example: a scientist only concerned about advancing knowledge, who does not respect the dignity of the human person, can easily turn the person into an object or a thing for the sole purpose of gaining knowledge. In the drive for medical progress and advancement it becomes all too easy to overlook the patient's dignity and the need to obtain his free and informed consent for medical experimentation. The "overlooking" of these moral safeguards is often rationalized by an appeal to "the benefits for future patients." However, such benefits cannot be obtained at any cost. The future cannot and will not be made more human by present actions and policies which are dehumanizing.

The privatization of ethics is accepted by many today as a mere fact of modern existence. Ever since the Enlightenment we have assumed that ethics, religion and the moral life are private and must be confined to the heart, home and house of worship. In the image of Lutheran theologian and pastor Richard Neuhaus, the public square must remain naked of religion and morality. If these two were to be admitted (of course they are present and will continue to be present though now they are often disguised and unrecognized) the result would be social violence, loss of civility and a renewal of religious wars that have been so much a part of man's history. Hence, if we are to maintain domestic tranquility we must confine religion and morality to very specific and private areas.

No matter how much we try, religion and moral choices continue to operate in the hospital, in the biology lab, in the Pentagon and in the halls of Congress. The great wall of separation between church and state; religion and politics; and values and social policy is filled with cracks. Questions of values leak through, over, and under this so-called Constitutional safeguard (the phrase "wall of separation" does not appear in the Constitution but in the correspondence of Thomas Jefferson). The debates about the national budget are more than dollars and cents; the allocation of resources by a society involves more than cold cash; the decisions that are made in lab and hospital ward involve more than scientific fact and medical knowledge. In all of these issues, and many more, values are in competition and various understandings of justice, fairness and the common good are in play.

The crucial issue becomes one of awareness. Our science and our ethics are ill served by the failure to unearth the moral issues lurking in abundance. Hence, the importance of ethics as "corrective vision" (May) for medicine and science. Such an approach seeks to remove the blindness which shuts out ethical concerns and sees issues in medicine and science as problems to be solved by the "value-free" method of scientific inquiry. In addition, if ethical reflection can help correct and purify our vision then it can also aid in the formation of a virtuous character. For ethical reflection is not merely concerned with what we are to do, but more importantly with who we are to become. The physician or the scientist is a human being first. The more one's humanity is developed as a caring, loving, competent and compassionate person the more effective one will be as a physician or scientist. Hence, medical education should be concerned with more than the accumulation of facts, the passing of courses, competence with diagnosis and treatment, and even a pleasing bedside manner. True education should purify and draw out the nobler aspects of one's humanity. Authentic education allows the physician to develop a sensitivity for the moral dimensions of ethical reflection.

What is Bio-ethics?

Former professional football coach George Allen was fond of saying, "The future is now." The on-rushing presence of the future is not confined to the football field. Rapid advances in medicine, biology and the entire field of the life sciences have brought the future into the present with shocking speed. Unfortunately we have not been able to keep our ethical reflections even with, or ahead of, our technological advances. Today we lack the time needed to reflect, evaluate and consult on the moral and social implications of our bio-medical advances. Too often what happens is this: a new technology or procedure becomes possible. Under pressure to be the first to perform a procedure, or if the life of a particular patient demands immediate action, we experiment. It is only *after* the procedure or test in the lab that we begin to ask questions of an ethical sort. By this time it is often too late. The questions of what *ought* to be done are deemed irrelevant or simply obstructionistic. We must move on. We must now turn our attention to perfecting or commercializing the given technology or procedure. The ethical issues are left further behind as a whole new set of issues waits to impact on our conscience and consciousness. We often experience a sense of powerlessness and bewilderment. The solution most often heard is this: let's not stand in the way of progress. Each individual will have to make a private choice as to whether one will use a given technology or procedure.

Bio-medical ethics is the discipline which seeks to reflect on the moral dimensions of the tremendous advances in the life sciences. Bioethics comes from the two Greek words *bio* and *ethos*. The word *bio* means life. The word *ethos* means the spirit or essence of a thing or person. Hence, we can define bioethics in the following way:

Bioethics is the reflection by the whole person (intellect, will, emotions, creative imagination) on the moral issues raised by the advances in bio-medical technology (hence the notion of corrective vision is crucial to highlight these moral dimensions). Furthermore, bioethics is vitally concerned with the formation of the moral character and the performance of individual acts by the physician and scientist which help to form such a character.

From this definition we can see that bioethics is not a special type of ethics unrelated to our traditional ethics. Bioethics is the application of our general ethical perspective to a specific area of human activity—medicine and the life sciences. What makes bioethics distinctive is the issues, questions and topics that come under consideration.

Bioethics covers an enormous range of topics (abortion, birth defects, death and dying, euthanasia, behavior modification, genetic engineering, human experimentation, organ transplantation, population control, reproductive technologies, patient rights, the quality of medical education, social justice and the allocation of resources, suicide) and a complicated assortment of questions: What is human life? What value do we place on human life? When can human life be termed "personal"? What is death? What are the acceptable criteria for death? How do we morally care for the dying? To what extent can/should we manipulate our genetic make-up? What are the basic rights of all patients? How should a society justly and fairly allocate its scarce resources of money, medicine, research and the like? What is essentially human about sexuality? How do the various reproductive technologies affect the family, marriage and human sexuality? How are we to protect the dignity of all human beings in the performance of various experiments, transplants and the modification of harmful or violent behavior? Because of the range of topics and the assortment of questions, bioethics follows a thoroughly *interdisciplinary* approach. The insights of the life sciences, humanities and the arts are sought if our reflections are to provide the depth needed. The interdisciplinary approach of bioethics is both a blessing and a curse. It is a curse in that the various disciplines can easily fall into competition rather than cooperation. It is a blessing in that we can work together as a community seeking to advance the physical, moral and spiritual life of the society. We come to realize that the complexity and profoundness of existence challenge us to share our insights as gifts and not selfish possessions.

Finally, while these issues are complex and the questions troubling, we cannot turn over our consciences and decision-making power to the experts. The issues of bio-medical ethics involve us all. We cannot step aside and relinquish our responsibility to question, be informed and make responsible decisions. After the professionals and experts have had their say, it is up to us to determine the road we must travel. The physician and scientist are able to inform us as to what *can* be done, but each of us must decide what *ought* to be done. Naturally, we listen to the experts so as to be informed. We need the input of professionals. We need to be schooled in our religious and moral tradition. Yet in the final analysis it is up to the individual to apply the knowledge and tradition (story, if you will) to the given case or issue under discussion.

To help our decision making in the area of bio-medical ethics we are fortunate to have three friends: our Catholic tradition in the area of medical ethics; the articulation of various principles that offer guidance for bio-medical decision making; and finally, the biblical view of human life in light of God's story of creation. Let us examine each of these in turn.

The Catholic Tradition

Catholic moralist Father Charles E. Curran of the Catholic University of America has written: "Medical ethics has occupied a prominent place in Catholic moral theology in the present century. In the United States alone, a proportionately large number of books has been written in this area. Furthermore, many of the utterances of recent popes have been concerned with the moral problems confronting modern medicine" (*Medicine and Morals*. Cf. Curran's *Catholic Moral Theology in Dialogue*, "Dialogue with Science: Scientific Data, Scientific Possibilities and the Moral Judgment"). There are a number of reasons why the Catholic moral tradition has been so prominent in the field of medical ethics. Let us briefly examine some of the more important factors.

1. The Catholic moral tradition (and Catholic theology in general) has constantly sought to befriend human reason. Catholic theology has understood itself as faith seeking understanding. Unlike some forms of Protestant theology, the Catholic tradition has not forced its members to choose faith over reason or even to understand reason as an enemy of faith. Father Charles E. Curran writes:

> . . . in theory it seems that Catholic moral theology has traditionally proposed a stance or posture which is open to the importance of the data of the sciences in the moral judgment . . . moral theology has never excluded the human and the rational from its considerations. The history of Roman Catholic thinking especially in the area of the relationship between Christian ethics and human ethics shows a willingness to enter into coalition with various forms of human and rational ethics. (*Dialogue with Science*)

This openness to the findings of science and the willingness to befriend human reason (Catholic theology has not shared the belief with Protestants that sin has corrupted everything and that human reason easily becomes intellectual pride) is clearly expressed by the Second Vatican Council in its document, *The Pastoral Constitution on the Church in the Modern World*: "Thanks to the experience of past ages, the progress of the sciences, and the treasure hidden in the various forms of human culture, the nature of man himself is more clearly revealed, and new roads for truth are opened. These benefits profit the Church."

2. Traditional Catholic moral theology has emphasized the importance of individual human acts (those characterized by reason and free will) in determining one's moral orientation. No aspect of human life is unimportant. Hence, an elaborate system of ethics was developed in order to satisfy the moral rightness and wrongness of individual acts. Each individual act carries with it a moral value that operates independently and objectively apart from the subjective intent or condition of the actor. This emphasis on human acts received philosophical and theological support from Aristotle and St. Thomas Aquinas. The Catholic moral tradition's (being greatly influenced by natural law) emphasis on individual acts and the formation of an elaborate ethical system has produced what is referred to as *casuistry*. Casuistry is often understood as an emphasis (or an overemphasis) on rules, principles and laws which are applied to every aspect of human behavior and the hard cases of morality. Casuistry is often accused of legalism and rigidity. However, Professor Stanley Hauerwas raises a voice of appreciation for this approach:

> Casuistry is the reflection by a community on its experience to test imaginatively the often unnoticed and unacknowledged implications of its narrative character . . . What I mean by casuistry, then, is not just the attempt to

adjudicate difficult cases of conscience within a system of moral principles, but is the process by which a tradition tests whether its practices are consistent (that is, truthful) or inconsistent in the light of its basic habits and convictions or whether these convictions require new practices and behavior. Those implications become apparent only through the day-to-day living of a people pledged to embody that narrative within their own lives.

(The Peaceable Kingdom)

In other words, human acts are anything but insignificant. For there is a story (a tradition) that serves to ground these acts. And what is more, our acts become experiments for testing the truth and trustworthiness of our foundational stories.

The Catholic community has a rich liturgical and sacramental system. The sacraments of Baptism and Extreme Unction (Sacrament of the Sick) involved the priest, loved ones and church as a whole in the questions of life, death and dying. The family needed to know when to call the priest. The priest had to know how to read "the signs of the body" in order to administer the sacraments at the crucial moment. The priest was drawn into the medical arena and contact with the medical community. The priest and the doctor needed to work together. Baptism needed to be administered to the newborn dying baby. Extreme Unction was administered to the dying patient. In order for this to be done doctor and priest, hospital and church had to come together for the healing and care of the patient.

In addition to these sacraments at the "edge of life," the Catholic Church had developed an elaborate penitential system which placed great importance on human acts (as we discussed above). As the Church began to expand and more converts were accepted into the community of faith, an elaborate system of sins and penances was formulated by Irish monks. In many ways this system and its emphasis on human acts remains with us today.

Emphasis was placed on regular confession with the enumera-
tion of sins and the number of times each was done. The
sacraments of Baptism, Penance and Extreme Unction highlighted the importance of life and death, the moral significance
of human acts, and the destiny and the dignity of the human
person beyond the confines of this world.

4. Finally, the great Catholic Christian symbols of creation,
incarnation, resurrection and indwelling of the Paraclete provide
us with an extraordinary view of the human body. God creates
the human person and breathes His life breath into the body
formed from the clay. The very spirit of God animates our
bodily existence. The Incarnation tells us that God became flesh,
became fully human in the person of Jesus of Nazareth. The
body is raised to a level of great dignity. The body is not to be
looked upon as a tomb which imprisons the soul. Rather, the
human body is the dwelling place of the Holy Spirit. Through
Baptism our body becomes a living tabernacle for the transforming, re-creating Spirit. The body that receives the Paraclete is
destined for glory through "the resurrection of the body." Our
corporeal existence is destined for the new creation and will be
transformed into the likeness of the risen Christ. St. Paul writes
to the Romans:

> For if we have been united with him in a death like his, we
> shall certainly be united with him in a resurrection like his
> . . . if we have died with Christ, we believe that we shall also
> live with him.   (Romans 6:5, 8)

These great symbols of our faith uphold the integrity of the body
and indicate that we are to reverence and promote our physical
well-being. Hence, these symbols can serve as a vital bridge
between religion and medicine in the ministry of healing.

Moral Principles in Bio-medical Ethics

The Catholic moral tradition, through centuries of reflection on human existence, has developed a number of valuable ethical principles which provide guidance for ethics in general and bio-medical ethics in particular. Before we examine these principles it would be helpful to offer a brief word about the importance *and* limitations of moral principles.

Our moral principles are not hard and fast rules which we can easily apply in an automatic way to every situation that confronts us. Moral principles do not always yield "clear and distinct" answers to complex questions. Moral principles serve as guidelines which help to structure a response for a particular case or situation. The temptation is to turn our moral principles into hitching-posts instead of sign-posts. We want to let the principles do the work of conscience, judgment and evaluation. The appeal to principles in a mechanistic fashion can give the illusion that the moral life is nothing but the application of principles. Such a view of the moral life breeds minimalism and overlooks the ambiguity and conflict that often arises in daily living.

The human condition is characterized by temporality, finitude, paradox, tragedy and sin. There is also grace, light and the indwelling presence of the Spirit. We experience an inner tension between the good we desire and the evil we often find ourselves doing. Hence, life and history are filled with the tragedy of having to choose between conflicting goods and lesser evils. Our principles and values find themselves in competition and downright conflict. For example, we often obtain much of our scientific knowledge and medical advances at the expense of the sick, the dying and the dead. Nothing comes cheaply. Therefore we need to be cautious in the application of our principles and be constantly vigilant for the need to modify and

creatively apply them. Father Richard A. McCormick, S.J.,
writes with great insight:

> . . . our choices are mixed, ambiguous. This intertwining of
> good and evil in our choices brings ambiguity into the
> world. The limitations of human beings become eventually
> the limitations of the world, and the limitations of the
> world return to us in the form of tragic conflict situations.
> Thus the good we do is rarely untainted by hurt, depriva-
> tion, imperfection. Our ethical acts are, at best, faint ap-
> proximations of the kingdom that is to come. We must kill
> to preserve life and freedom; we protect one through the
> pain of another; our education must at times be punitive;
> our health is preserved at times by pain and disfiguring
> mutilation; we protect our secrets by misstatements and
> our marriages and population by contraception and sterili-
> zation.   (*Health and Medicine in the Catholic Tradition*)

If we keep in mind the above mentioned limitations and ambiguity of our principles and the human condition, we will not ask
more of our principles than they are able to yield. This moral
realism can do much to shield us from a legalism which expects
principles to solve all of our problems in a neat fashion.
Likewise, we are saved from a despair that abandons all principles and settles moral issues on the basis of feelings and private
choices. Let us now examine four (4) moral principles that are
crucial in the study of bio-medical ethics.

   1. *The sanctity of human life*. Human life is a fundamental
and basic value. All values (love, justice, fidelity, etc.) pass from
the realm of abstraction to the realm of concrete existence
because living human beings *do* values. The values of love,
justice and fidelity have meaning because there are loving, just
and faithful human beings. Without upholding the primary

value of human life, all other values are placed in serious jeopardy.

A crucial point must be made, and cannot be over emphasized, that human life is *not* an absolute good but a primary good. God alone is the highest good and the supreme good or end of all existence. The Roman Catholic moral tradition has recognized instances in which human life can be sacrificed or taken, however regrettably, in light of other values. For example: the defense of one's own life or that of an innocent third party, which results in the unintended death of the aggressor; the taking of life by the state as punishment for those who commit capital offenses; and the development of a just-war theory which allows the killing of an unjust aggressor in order to defend one's life and institutions, and those of an innocent third party. In all of these instances, and many others, life is held to be a primary but not an absolute value. Father Richard A. McCormick, S.J. puts it succinctly: "Life is a basic good but not an absolute one . . . It is not *absolute* because there are higher goods for which life can be sacrificed (for example, the glory of God, the salvation of souls, or the service of one's brethren)."

2. *Ordinary/Extraordinary means of prolonging life.* These categories are crucial in the Catholic moral tradition concerning the issues of death and dying. Some of the most agonizing questions we face are related to death and dying in this revolutionary biological and technological age: When does one stop treatment of a patient? When do we initiate treatment in the first place? Ought we to do all we can do in a given situation to prolong life (of the dying)? What are the limits of our duty to prolong life? The categories of *ordinary* and *extraordinary* try to help us in making these difficult decisions. These *moral* categories were articulated by Pope Pius XII in a talk given to the International Congress of Anesthesiologists (1952):

A more strict obligation would be too burdensome for most

men and would render the attainment of the higher, more important good too difficult. Life, health, all temporal activities are in fact subordinated to spiritual ends.

Let us examine each of these important categories of prolonging human life.

Ordinary means. Ordinary means are all those treatments, operations and medicines which offer the patient a reasonable hope of benefit and recovery. Ordinary means are those which *do not* cause undue pain or inconvenience which destroy greater spiritual values. (Unfortunately these greater spiritual values were left unarticulated by Pius XII. However, some contemporary theologians have suggested love, interpersonal relationships, personal dignity and freedom.) An example of ordinary means would be the use of surgery such as an appendectomy in order to restore one to health. There is pain and inconvenience but it is a part of the healing process that one accepts in order to return to normal functioning.

Extraordinary means. Extraordinary means are all those medicines, operations and treatments which cannot be employed without undue pain, expense, inconvenience or reasonable hope of benefit and recovery. It must be emphasized that one is *not* obligated to employ such means to prolong life. However, one *can* do so if one wishes. The decision of the patient, when possible, is of primary importance. We may think that a given means is excessive; however, this is not what is crucial. For we know that people of good will and intelligence can disagree on the use of various means. What is crucial is this: to respect the responsible, free and informed decision of the conscious patient concerning the various means to be used in his or her treatment. An example of extraordinary means would be the use of a kidney dialysis machine on a patient for whom such a technology would place an undue burden. This burden could be experienced in terms of pain, inconvenience, isolation, rebellion against God, financial burdens and strain on one's family. In such a case the dialysis technology could be more of a burden than a treatment or an enhancement for living.

The distinction between ordinary and extraordinary means of prolonging life highlights a significant number of insights to help in bio-medical decision making. Among these insights four (4) bear mentioning.

a) The categories of ordinary and extraordinary are *moral* categories and not medical or technological categories. By this we mean that the decision as to what constitutes ordinary/extraordinary is to be determined by the patient (or next of kin or someone with the power of substituted judgment) and his or her situation. These categories are based on the physical, spiritual, emotional and financial well-being of the patient and the family. These categories are *not* based on the medical state of the art or the decision by the physician as to whether he considers a procedure ordinary or extraordinary. Again, the categories are *moral* and not technological.

b) These categories are crucial if we are to avoid *both* medical pessimism and medical vitalism. Medical pessimism holds that life is an individual possession that can be terminated when one no longer wishes to suffer no matter how reasonable the suffering may be for the healing process. Also, if one determines that life is too much of a burden or is not of sufficient quality, then life can be terminated. The pessimist view holds that suffering is the greatest evil. By contrast, medical vitalism holds physical, biological life to be the highest good. *All means* are considered ordinary and must be used in order to prolong life. As we indicated earlier Pope Pius XII and the Catholic moral tradition wisely reject both of these extremes.

c) The categories of ordinary/extraordinary are an important way of avoiding both slippery slope subjectivism and medicalism. These categories seek to place the delicate decisions of life and death on an *objective plane* which is sensitive to one's real needs while avoiding basing such decisions on one's feelings or the whims (and expediencies) of others. Also these categories serve as a safeguard against the too eager or defensive physician who considers all medical technology as ordinary or demanded by law in order not to be sued. These categories seek to protect the dignity of the patient and the freedom of his or her decisions.

d) Finally, the distinction between ordinary and extraordinary means of prolonging life, and the moral limits for such prolongation, remind us that bodily, physical life is not an absolute, ultimate good to be preserved at all cost. There are limits to our duty to cure. Our technology and medical know-how is finite. There comes a time when machines must step aside, for it is time to go with dignity into that mysterious night. Yet the Christian holds that the mysterious night of death gives way to the greater mystery of that new day when we are received forever into the Unbounded Love of God. The temptation today is to cease caring when we can no longer cure. However, as the distinguished Protestant moralist Paul Ramsey reminds us, there are limits to our curing but never to our caring. The canons of loyalty we owe to the sick and dying are especially strong at the times when they are weakest and most vulnerable.

3. *The Principle of Double Effect.* We live in a fallen world where there are seldom, if ever, any perfect solutions to our problems. Conflict and tragedy are all too common in our everyday experience. We see through a glass only darkly. A group of Catholic theologians, ethicists and health care professionals developed a document entitled, "Ethical Guidelines for Catholic Health Care Institutions," in which they state: ". . . the best way to care in particular circumstances is not always perfectly clear, since values often come into conflict with one another." The principle of double effect recognizes and takes seriously the tragedy and conflict of human existence. Very often we perform an action which produces two effects—one good and one evil. We desire the good but reject the evil. Unfortu-

nately the good and evil effects are inseparable. The question arises: may we seek the good even if the evil effect occurs? The answer is *YES* provided we adhere to the following guidelines:

    a) The action performed, in itself, must not be evil.

    b) The evil that results must not be a means to achieve the good effect. The end does not justify the use of any means.

    c) The evil effect *cannot be intended but only permitted or tolerated.* The *primary intention* of the moral agent is the good effect and the agent simply, *regrettably tolerates* the evil effect. This principle holds even when one can predict the evil effect.

    d) Finally, there must be a proportionate good reason for doing the act which balances the negative or evil effects. The good must at least be equal to or greater than the evil effect.

This fourth point, proportionate reason, can cause a great deal of difficulty because of the need to balance the good and bad effects. Such balancing and judging is by no means easy nor can it be done with sweet certainty. Father Richard A. McCormick, S.J. offers three insights in helping to clarify proportionate reasoning:

    1. Proportionate reason must be understood as the balancing of values that are of equal importance. In order to sacrifice one value we must at the same time uphold another value or values of equal importance.

    2. In sacrificing a value we do so only as a last resort and there must be no less harmful way of achieving the values we are seeking. We do the least possible harm.

    3. When we sacrifice a value in a given situation it should be understood that such a sacrifice may *not* apply in the future when other cases arise. We do not want to undermine the value. The long-range effects on values must be carefully considered.

These three insights of clarification concerning proportionate reason remind us that we seldom, if ever, enjoy absolute certainty in our moral decisions. There will always be an element of ambiguity and uncertainty. Moral decisions are more than the simple adding up of goods and evils. We must be sensitive to consequences, intentions and the development of the mature Christian conscience. Responsible moral behavior involves us in making decisions and standing by the consequences. This is seldom easy but always necessary.

4. *The Principle of Totality*. This principle states that the individual parts of the body exist for the sake (well-being) of the whole organism. St. Thomas Aquinas applied this principle for the justification of the removal of a diseased limb or part of the body. The formal presentation of totality as a principle of moral theology was made by Pius XII in 1952. He delivered an address entitled, "Allocution to the First International Congress of Histopathology" in which he spoke about the well-being of the human person "as a whole." The principle of totality is very important in the discussions surrounding amputations, the removal of diseased organs, and more recently the proliferation of human experimentation, organ transplants and organ donor procedures. Hence it becomes permissible to have surgery when the health and overall well-being of the whole body is at risk. The removal of a diseased organ or limb is morally required since without such actions the person would die. In terms of a living donor providing an organ for someone the *official* Church teaching is as follows: One can donate only paired organs (for example, a kidney) and parts of the body which regenerate (blood, bone marrow and tissue). However, healthy organs cannot be mutilated or amputated. The health of the whole organism would be jeopardized.

In recent times some theologians have sought to expand the principle of totality in such a way as to allow for the donation of healthy organs in order to benefit another who is sick or dying.

These theologians propose such an expansion on the grounds of the social and spiritual aspects of the human person. We are social beings who are called to live in a caring way with our brothers and sisters. We are called by Jesus to love one another and be of service to our neighbor in need. Hence, in order to be true to the community and service dimensions of our life we can donate a healthy organ out of love for one another. The principle of totality reminds us of the importance and dignity of the human body. Part of the gift of life is our corporeal existence which we are called to reverence and respect. Our body is not something we own but a gift we receive. Father McCormick reminds us, "the person is a bodily subject. Corporeality is essential to, and therefore shares in the excellence and dignity of, the human person."

The sacredness and dignity of human life is not merely contained in Catholic theology and Church documents. It is emphasized throughout the pages of Scripture. Man enjoys a special, unique relationship with God. In bringing this first chapter to a close let us examine the biblical view of life and the special relationship the human person enjoys with God.

The Bible and the Gift of Life

The opening pages of the Bible witness to the sacredness and special character of human life.

> Then God said: "Let us make man in our image, after our likeness" . . . God created man in his image; in the divine image he created him; male and female he created them.
> (Genesis 1:26, 27)
>
> . . . the Lord God formed man out of the clay of the ground and blew into his nostrils the breath of life, and so man became a living being. (Genesis 2:7)

The human person is made in the image and called to grow into the likeness of God. The source of human life, that which redeems, sustains and transforms that life, is God himself. The dignity and glory of the human person is not an achievement or a prize we grasp but a loving gift from God. The sacredness of human life ultimately turns our attention to God. All human beings are to be respected and protected because of the relationship we enjoy with the loving Father. The renowned German theologian and pastor Helmut Thielicke writes in his excellent book, *Being Human . . . Becoming Human*, the following:

> . . . we do not speak about a dignity of humanity that is based on qualities but about an "alien dignity" in Luther's sense. We humans are the apple of God's eye. Those who touch us, touch him. Our worth is based upon this imparted sharing in the divine life. The history with himself to which God has called us constitutes the basis, good, and meaning of our existence. It is the secret of our identity.

A group of bio-medical scholars from the Pope John XXIII Medical-Moral Research and Education Center have written the following about the dignity of human life because of its special gift, God's very life breath, at creation:

> The Bible says a great deal about man, but it concentrates on God and on getting man to concentrate on God. It does not attempt to study man for the sake of studying what makes up a human being, but for the sake of showing what makes up man's relationship to God.
> (*Handbook On Critical Life Issues*)

The special relationship of man to God fills one with a sense of awe. The God of creation and the Lord of life does not merely create and then forget His handiwork. God creates and calls that creation to Himself. In a special way the human person is called to continue the creative, life-giving work of the One in whose image we are wonderfully made. All that we are, do and hope to become bears the mark of the God who spoke us into history. The inviolability of human life does not come from one's bankbook, achievements, beauty, power, or one's contributions to the common good of society. In the words of Professor Thielicke, "Our dignity and inviolability is that we come from the hands of the Creator and that these hands are upon our lives and direct them until they go back to the one from whom they came." We may call this "alien dignity." The dignity of man fills the Psalmist with awe:

> What is man that you should be mindful of him, or the son of man that you should care for him?
> You have made him little less than the angels, and crowned him with glory and honor. You have given him rule over the works of your hands. . . .
> O Lord, our Lord,
> how gracious is your name over all the earth!
>
> (Psalm 8:5-7, 10)

The special relationship of the human person to God and the subsequent alien dignity is present from the beginning. How do we know that the unborn enjoys this special relationship and alien dignity? We cannot know this through the methods of science. All of this escapes our powers of analysis, measurement, and objectification. We are faced with the greatest of mysteries in which the authentic response is trust in the unbounded love of God. In fact, the Bible speaks of a relationship that we enjoy with God before conception. The Psalmist writes:

> O Lord, you have probed me and you know me; you know when I sit and when I stand; . . . Truly you have formed my

> inmost being; you knit me in my mother's womb . . . My
> soul you knew full well; nor was my frame unknown to you
> when I was made in secret, when I was fashioned in the
> depths of the earth. Your eyes have seen my actions; in
> your book they are written; my days were limited before
> one of them existed.   (Psalm 139:1-2, 13, 15-16)

The prenatal existence of human life and its relationship with
God is powerfully expressed in the biblical stories of the births of
John and Jesus. St. Luke tells us in his Gospel that Zechariah and
Elizabeth will have a son who is to be named John and "he will be
filled with the Holy Spirit from his mother's womb." Luke goes
on to recount the annunciation of Jesus' birth. This child of Mary
will be conceived through the power of the Holy Spirit and He
will be the Son of God (Lk 1:5-45). The words of the Psalmist,
the vocation of Jeremiah ("Before I formed you in the womb I
knew you, before you were born I dedicated you, a prophet to the
nations I appointed you" (Jr 1:5), and the annunciations of the
births of John and Jesus tell us, "We live in the thought of God
even before we are" (Thielicke).

Our dignity and special relationship with God is not only
prenatal, nor for this life only; but for all eternity. The covenant
relationship we have with God, formed by the redeeming love of
Jesus, is written on our hearts. Death does not end our relationship but through death we pass into the unbounded love of our
heavenly Father. The God who calls us into existence and
sustains us through the Spirit, is the God who calls our name for
all eternity. In the words of Luther: "Those with whom God has
begun to speak, whether in wrath or in grace, are immortal." The
love of God calls, sustains and remains faithful into eternity.
God does not brush aside those who are made into His image
and likeness. St. Paul, writing to the Romans, beautifully
captures the everlasting quality of our relationship with God in
Christ:

None of us lives as his own master and none of us dies as his own master. While we live we are responsible to the Lord, and when we die we die as his servants. Both in life and in death we are the Lord's. That is why Christ died and came to life again, that he might be Lord of both the dead and the living. (Romans 14:7-9)

The loving voice that calls us into existence is the same loving voice that calls us through the shadows of the valley of death into the light of life eternal.

Summary and Transition

The following are the essential points we have advanced in this foundational chapter:

1. Christian ethics is concerned with both character formation and the moral quality of the acts we perform. Both character (the question of being) and moral acts (the question of doing) are understood in light of our stories about Israel and Jesus: that life is a gift from God; that all human beings are made in the image and likeness of God; that we are called to share forever the unbounded love of God.

2. There is no such thing as value-free or neutral science. Human values are at work in every decision we make in the fields of science and medicine. It is crucial that our ethical reflection helps to impart to us a "corrective vision" whereby we "see" the values that are at work, are in conflict and are challenged.

3. Bioethics is a subdivision of general ethics whereby we apply our stories, principles, values and virtues to the issues of medicine, science and the life sciences as a whole. The Catholic moral tradition has a long history of reflection on medical-moral problems. This interest in medical ethics is due to Catholicism's befriending of human reason; its emphasis on individual acts

that are morally significant; and its rich liturgical and sacramental traditions. Finally, Catholic theology as a whole has upheld the dignity of the body because of Christ's Incarnation and Resurrection, and His sending of the indwelling Spirit.

4. Catholic moral theology in the field of medicine has relied heavily on four (4) fundamental principles: the sanctity of human life; the distinction between ordinary and extraordinary means of prolonging life; the principle of double effect; and the principle of totality. These principles are not to be used as hitching-posts but as sign-posts. They help us, but never replace our conscience and the need for personal judgment and responsibility, as guidelines in facing difficult cases.

5. Finally, the biblical view of human life proclaims that it is a gift from our loving God. All human beings are created in the image of God and are called to grow into the divine likeness. The dignity of each person is "alien," that is, it is not earned but given by God because of our special relationship. Earthly life is not the end of our existence. We are made for glory and are called to share the divine life for eternity.

We will now turn our attention to three of the most troubling issues facing us as Catholics, as Christians and, with increasing urgency, as citizens of the United States. These are the problems of abortion, euthanasia and suicide. In our discussions we hope to avoid slogans which produce more heat than light. We do not want our voice to become shrill and judgmental. At the same time, we want to hold fast to our belief in the sacredness of human life and the need to defend and enhance this great gift from God. We hope that what follows will befit the compassion of Christ, the thoughtfulness of the Catholic tradition, and the transforming grace of the Holy Spirit. In other words, that the reflections which follow will be a blessing and advance the day all God's children are welcomed in *this* world as they are in heaven.

II

Abortion: For Whom DOES The Bell Toll?

Back to Basics

It was late one afternoon after a rather long day of teaching classes and coaching girls' basketball (I am not sure which is the tougher). A professional colleague and friend approached with small talk and innocent conversation (a sure sign to get ready for action). Finally, as the talk got smaller and the silence between topics became more pronounced and awkward, I asked, "Jane, what's really up with you? What do you really want to talk about?" After a brief embarrassed smile Jane came out with it. "Bill, I have a friend who's visiting me and she really needs to talk to someone. She needs to talk with a priest." After catching her breath she continued, "I was hoping . . . I felt she. . ." "Jane," I said, "I'll be happy to talk with your friend. However, can't you tell me what this is all about?"

Jane spent a few moments pressing her fingers together and looking down at the floor. Finally she said, "I really can't bring myself to tell you about it. It's got to come from Anne. She's the one who must tell you." I must admit I felt a bit uneasy about this mysterious, and obviously quite upsetting, situation. However, I told Jane I would see Anne that night at seven-thirty at the parish rectory. Jane thanked me and left the room as if an enormous burden had been lifted. I left feeling as if one had just been applied.

I was a bit nervous waiting for Anne to arrive. Finally seven-thirty arrived but Anne did not. It was now ten minutes to eight and still no Anne. I was about to call Jane or just go upstairs and call it a night when the doorbell rang. It was Anne. And she was not what I had expected.

I had expected a woman out of an Alfred Hitchock movie—desperate, secretive, and a little out of breath. Anne was none of these. She was about thirty-eight (later I found out she was all of forty!), well dressed, polite, and very much in control on the surface. She tried very hard to remain in control of the situation, and especially of her feelings.

She began by thanking me for seeing her on such short notice. We discussed her visiting with Jane and how she (Anne) would be returning home in a day or two. Once again I found myself moving the conversation to more substantive areas. "Anne," I said, "Jane tells me that something is troubling you and she thinks I might be able to help."

Before I was able to go any further Anne said, "Yes, it's now or never. I've waited about twenty years to speak with someone, a priest, about my situation. I can no longer wait. Here goes." All the while Anne was speaking it was as if she had rehearsed these lines for years just for the right occasion (something like the prodigal son in Luke's Gospel). Also, I had the impression that Anne was about to begin her story for someone in addition to the two of us. An unseen third person was present.

Anne took a deep breath and began: "Father Maestri, I was a junior at a large college in the East. I am originally from a small town in the Mid-West and college life was not what I expected. The school is very prestigious. The students are sophisticated and fast. I was a hick from the sticks. I wanted so much to belong and be accepted. I drank and smoked (no heavy drugs—I did a lot of faking at parties). I met a boy who was everything to me then. Especially he was everything I wasn't; and like no one back home." For a brief moment a distant look came across Anne's face. Then she pulled herself back into the present and went on.

"More and more I grew to depend upon Rick. I think he knew it and used it to control me." There was a strong sense of bitterness in Anne's face and voice. She continued, "One day, for the first time, he told me he loved me. He wanted us to move in together." The bitterness was softened in tone and even a brief smile came to Anne's face. Anne went on: "Father, I really think I loved him. I know I did. I thought he loved me. So we moved in together. Life was great. Then it happened." Anne's voice went very soft and her head was bent and she stared down at the floor. "I became pregnant. When I told Rick he was furious. He said that unless I got an abortion we were through. He didn't want to be a father. I was certainly not prepared to be a mother." Anne was now fighting with all her strength to hold back the tears and the anger. It was no use. She had lost control and was sobbing with deep emotion. After several minutes she was able to continue her story.

"I didn't go right away. I went to the church to pray. However, I knew what I was planning so I quickly ran out. How could God help me when I was considering an abortion? I asked certain friends for help. I was desperate. I loved Rick. I also loved this new life in me." Anne seemed all cried out. Her tone was now "matter of fact." It was as if, as a defense mechanism, she had shifted into the third person. It was her words, story and pain. Yet it was as if she were listening to the story of another.

"Finally Rick drove me to the clinic. It was the worst day ever. I was afraid and lonely. I didn't want what was about to happen. But it did. I had the abortion. Rick picked me up. I was in a state of depression for weeks. I didn't eat, communicate or go to class. I felt everyone knew what I had done. I felt guilty, angry at feeling guilty, and very unclean."

I asked Anne what became of her relationship with Rick. She told me they "split." He dropped out of school. Anne graduated (with the help of friends) and married. She told me she has three children and a wonderful husband who does *not* know about her past. She is a very successful public relations executive for a large investment firm. She has started going to church again and prays daily. Anne also indicated to me that "not a day goes by that I do not think of my first child. I remember his birthday every year." (She said she always hoped her first child would be a boy.)

I asked Anne why after so many years she had decided to speak with a priest and seek reconciliation. Anne said, "I need forgiveness. I don't want anyone to say what I did was right. I don't think it was. I just need to know that I have been forgiven. I want to come back to the Church. I don't know how this sounds, but I need to say 'Amen' to the 'Body of Christ.' It's time to heal the past."

I beg the reader's indulgence in relating this story. It instructs us about the issue of abortion. For abortion is fundamentally about people; about flesh and blood human beings who face some of the most wrenching decisions they will ever have to make. The "human factor" can so easily be lost in the heat and rhetoric of today's debate. However, the Christian story proclaims the primacy of the human. The stories of the creation, and of the Incarnation and healing ministry of Jesus are powerful reminders that "the glory of God is man fully alive." Our moral principles and values are means toward that end—to give glory to God by helping His creatures become fully alive.

As I listened to Anne with her story about abortion, I felt that the images of the media distort much of life. Abortion is a "hot topic" for any morning news or discussion program. Both sides muster their arguments in hopes of winning points and "coming across" as reasonable or compassionate. Usually the show disintegrates into all parties shouting at once. More often than not, the program is filled with tapes of marching crowds, shouting groups outside abortion clinics, preachers preaching, and law-makers trying to be statesman-like. We are left with the impression that this is what abortion is all about—competing values, marching crowds, shouting groups, and various voices that speak *at* us in hopes of providing some light. The result is predictable. We are left with more confusion and anger than before. We feel a great (or not so great) sense of powerlessness. Finally, we come to feel that abortion is a "private choice" and that the best way to maintain civil order is to let the decision remain there. Maybe it will go away.

Yet the reality of abortion is quite different. The story and feelings of Anne are closer to the truth. There is an enormous amount of pain, anger, depression, alienation and soul searching. In other words, there is a tremendous need for teaching, conversion and compassion. The healing and teaching ministries of the Church are greatly challenged by abortion. Our moral identity as a nation is revealed by the ways we value life—especially the life of those on the margins of our society: the weak, sick and poor. Abortion is the issue *par excellence* which reveals our deepest values and most cherished hopes. Father Richard A. McCormick, S.J. has insightfully captured the essence and challenge of the abortion issue:

> Abortion is a matter that is morally problematic, pastorally delicate, legislatively thorny, constitutionally insecure, ecumenically divisive, medically normless, humanly anguishing, racially provocative, journalistically abused, personally biased, and widely performed. It demands a most extraordinary discipline of moral thought, one that is penetrating without being impenetrable, humanly compassionate without being morally compromising, legally realistic without being legally positivistic, instructed by cognate disciplines without being determined by them, informed by tradition without being enslaved by it . . . Abortion, therefore, is a severe testing ground for moral reflection. Abortion is probably a paradigm of the way we will face other

problems in the future. Many of us are bone-weary of the subject, but we cannot afford to indulge this fatigue.

("The Abortion Dossier," *How Brave A New World?*)

From what Father McCormick says, abortion sets before us a kind of ethical "mission impossible." However, bone-weary or not, we must continue to reflect and struggle with this paradigm issue. There is too much at stake to merely turn our attention to less troubling issues. Our Christian responsibility for helping to build a more just, peaceable and free world will not allow us to be excused. It is for people like Anne, and countless others like her, that we continue to witness to the sacredness of life from womb to tomb and all points in between. If we find ourselves growing "bone-tired" let us be renewed by the words of Isaiah:

> They who wait for the Lord shall renew their strength,
> they shall mount up with wings like eagles,
> they shall run and not be weary,
> they shall walk and not faint.   (Isaiah 40:31)

We will begin this chapter by discussing the medical aspects of abortion, including the various kinds of abortion along with a brief discussion concerning the medical "reasons" for abortion. Then we shall turn our attention to the highly complex legal developments that have surrounded abortion. Of special concern will be the relationship between the legal and the moral. Abortion has become one of the most debated issues in our society, and we will examine the role of the Catholic in such public debates. Of course, abortion extends beyond the medical, legal and political arenas. Abortion offers us the opportunity to review our deepest held values about human life and what our biblical faith and moral tradition hold as foundational. Hence, we want to present the magisterial teaching about abortion along with some of the reflections of modern moralists. We will bring this chapter to a close with some pastoral reflections on how to minister to those who have had abortions or who are considering abortion.

Medical Aspects of Abortion

In chapter one we indicated that Catholic theology understands itself as "faith seeking understanding." At least in theory, it exhibits an openness to science and the faculty of human reason. Hence, our discussions concerning abortion (and the whole of medical ethics) must pay serious (but not exclusive) attention to an excellent publication of the Pope John Center, *Handbook On Critical Life Issues* (see chapter 8, "Abortion in Medicine and Ethics").

What is the medical definition of abortion? Abortion is understood as the birth of the child before he or she can live outside the womb (before viability). There are two general types of abortions: induced and natural or spontaneous. The *induced* abortion is understood as the purposeful expulsion of the child from the mother's womb. These induced or planned abortions consist of two general approaches: the child is killed while in the womb or the abortion results from a willful premature birth in which the child is allowed to die. The second type of abortion is termed *natural* or spontaneous (also called a miscarriage) and occurs because of a defect either of the placenta or of the baby which causes a premature birth resulting in death.

The landmark Supreme Court decision of Roe v. Wade has made the language of "trimesters" when discussing pregnancy widely acceptable. Hence, we can speak of the first, second and third trimester at which intervals various considerations come into play in the abortion decision. Let us briefly examine the three types of abortions performed during these various trimesters of pregnancy.

First trimester abortions. There are two types of abortions usually performed during these early months—so called D & C (dilation and curettage) and S & C (suction curettage). The D & C procedure requires a dilation of the cervix and a scraping of the lining of the womb with an instrument called a curette. The scraping and cutting affects the placenta and the baby. It is not unusual for the baby to be dismembered. All parts of the dismembered baby must be accounted for since any part left inside the womb would cause severe bleeding and infection.

The so called S & C procedure involves the placing of a tube into the uterus and sucking (by means of a vacuum) the tissues and baby into a bottle. Once again the bottle must be checked for the baby's members in order to insure that all parts have been removed. There is a variation of the S & C (a mini-abortion) called a menstrual extraction. However, this abortion is performed very early in the pregnancy (2 or 3 weeks). In fact there are no discernable parts of the child visible to the eye.

Second trimester abortions. Once again there are two types of abortions performed during this period: instillation abortions and "dilation and evacuation" (D & E). The instillation abortion involves the placing of a needle into the womb for the purpose of withdrawing some amniotic fluid and the injection of a saline solution or drugs called prostaglandins. The prostaglandins induce the womb to contract so the child will be expelled from the womb prematurely so as to die (a very tragic situation arises when the child is expelled still breathing). The hypertonic saline solution causes womb contraction and severe burns to the baby. The baby is expelled from the womb. However, as with the case of the prostaglandins abortion, a baby can be born alive. Some medical experts are of the opinion that a baby in the second trimester can feel and react to pain. None of these procedures is pain free.

The second type of abortion performed during the second trimester is termed D & E. Like the D & C, the D & E involves the dilation of the cervix (this is done by metal dilation or the use of *Laninaria*—a seaweed species which causes cervix dilation) and the use of special forceps which remove the placenta, membranes and the child from the uterus. The baby is crushed with the ovum forceps so that removal can take place without damaging the cervix. Of course, all parts of the baby must be removed in order to avoid infection and hemorrhage.

Third trimester abortions. During the last three months the child may be too large for various scraping procedures to be performed. The physician may employ an instillation procedure or turn to a more radical procedure—a hysterectomy. Naturally the child is not saved even when born alive (the baby is usually born alive). While there are rare occasions in which the child survives, more often it dies because the respiratory system lacks the maturation necessary to support life outside the womb.

Abortion procedures are not deadly only for the child in the womb. Even in the present American context of legal abortion, the side effects of induced abortions for the mother, as well as the medical staff are no small matter. For example, as we have mentioned throughout our discussion of various abortion techniques there is a real danger of infection and hemorrhage. Many women have died while undergoing legal abortions in hospitals and clinics. It is difficult to obtain exact figures on the number of abortion-related deaths for the women. One thing we are able to report is this: during 1984 there were 1.5 million abortions performed in America. Of these legal abortions the Center for Disease Control reports that 1% of the women suffered severe complications. The CDC goes on to report that of the women who had abortions 10% experienced some form of medical complication. What we are unable to determine at this point is the long-range effects of abortions (especially multiple abortions) on subsequent pregnancies. For some women an abortion may prevent future pregnancies or may cause miscarriages.

The side effects of abortion are not limited to the physical.

There are varying degrees of psychological trauma for the woman (one woman who had an abortion told me, "There isn't a day that goes by I don't think of *my baby*. This is especially true when I pass a schoolyard or receive an invitation to a baptism. I carry a terrible burden.") and for the members of the medical staff (this is especially true since their training is for healing and life). One nurse who once worked in an abortion clinic told me "I only stayed there (in the clinic) two days. On the third day I got up and knew I couldn't be a nurse and do abortions. I am very sorry for the women who come to these clinics."

Abortion has special trauma for the often forgotten father. In the whole noisy controversy over abortion, the feelings of the father are ignored as irrelevant. However, as one father told me, "I've never felt so powerless in all my life. The depression and anger really worry me. The trouble is, I am not sure I have the *right* to feel this way. She never even asked what I wanted. I felt I didn't have the *right* to voice my feelings." In all of these voices we clearly see the human anguish that highlights the folly of abortion as "a private choice."

In bringing this section on medical aspects of abortion to a close, it is important to keep in mind the following when discussing the so-called "hard cases" concerning abortion: "Due to modern medical advances, there are no medical conditions in which abortion is absolutely recommended." Of course pregnancy does not exclude one from kidney or heart disease, or high blood pressure. Pregnancy can be severely handicapped by these conditions, and pregnancy can aggravate these diseases. There is an unfortunate "rush to abortion" by some physicians. However, as the research group at the Pope John Center remind us:

> It should be emphasized that patients with the rather rare conditions listed above (severe kidney disease, lung disease, diabetes, and various forms of cancer such as phenochaomocytoma [a tumor which secretes adrenol-like

hormones] and a ruptured tube in the ectopic pregnancy) are at somewhat higher risk for developing complications during pregnancy than are otherwise healthy women. They need good medical care during their pregnancy. In addition, it is now recognized by physicians that pregnancy does not cause as serious a burden on the body during disease as once was thought. So, it would seem that the vast majority of women, even those afflicted with serious diseases, can survive pregnancy.

(Handbook on Critical Life Issues)

There is another group of "hard cases" which make for "hard choices." Namely, pregnancy is not always the result of a loving sharing between husband and wife. We know all too well the specter of domestic and sexual violence in our society. The publicity given to cases of rape and incest heighten our sensitivity and outrage at such violence. Many people believe that it is best to have an abortion in cases of rape and incest. In addition to the physical violence done to the woman, she would be expected to carry a nine month reminder of the terrible episode(s). This only adds insult to injury and prolongs the victimization of the female. Furthermore, a woman who has been raped or is the victim of incest may very likely commit suicide if required to carry the child of violence to term. Hence, abortion is considered as both acceptable and moral.

What is one to make of this? Certainly the tragedy and suffering are real. Victims abound in such situations: the woman, the unborn child in the womb, loved ones, society as a whole. Even the rapist is often a victim of child abuse. The question is: do we perpetuate the violence? Abortion is a perpetuation of the violence against the weak, voiceless and unprotected. The unborn child is similar to the woman who was attacked, except that the child in the womb cannot claim its rights to due process (the unborn have no rights). The unborn child is voiceless and totally dependent upon others to plead its cause. The tragedy of incest and rape is continued in abortion.

Won't the woman who is "forced" to carry an unwanted pregnancy commit suicide or perform some type of violence so as to induce abortion herself? Surprisingly, or not so surprisingly, the answer *seems* to be no. I say "seems" because we do not have clear evidence to the contrary. In fact, there are indications that carrying the pregnancy to term may actually foster feelings of protection, strength and personal resolve in the woman. If I might risk being labeled a chauvinist pig, the mothering, nurturing instinct or response is brought out in such situations. From a theological point of view might we not even risk going so far as to call such situations of heroic acceptance moments of grace? The acceptance of the unacceptable is much akin to the Paschal Mystery of dying and rising with the Lord. In all honesty, it must be said that it is easy to say this, difficult to live with.

What we have said about the hard cases of incest and rape can likewise be applied to the genetically defective unborn child. The use of prenatal testing (for example, the use of amniocentesis) for the early detection of genetic defects is most helpful in preparing for the birth of the child and its proper care afterwards. While we can tell that a child has certain defects, we can never be sure of the degree of retardation or the severity of the handicap. These are often only known *after* the child is born and begins to actualize his or her potential. Unfortunately, the "solution" of abortion is appealing. Such abortions are often done in the name of high principles—a life not worth living; a life of useless suffering; a life not of sufficient quality; no one would really want to live in that condition; and the list goes on and on. However, what is often lost is the value of the unborn child and his or her right to life. The defective child is still one made in the image and likeness of God. The defective child is still a brother or sister in Christ. If the defective unborn is imperfect, weak and in special need that is just another way of saying that Jesus in His need has come to us once again. For if unborn and genetically defective children in the womb are the least of our brothers and sisters, then they are at the same time privileged occasions to meet Christ. We stand on holy ground!

Bioethicist William F. May once wrote that the unborn child is not a potential human being but a human being with potential. The humanity is already present. It will unflower if allowed to do so free from external and internal damage along with the proper nurturing and love. Hence, it will be most helpful to conclude this section on the medical aspects of abortion by presenting a time table of child development while in the uterus:

AGE	What takes place
1 day	The union of egg and sperm forms the zygote, the beginning of the new individual. The first cell division of the zygote, the first step in its growth, is completed within 36 hours. By future cell division (mitosis) all the cells and tissues of the new individual will arise from the zygote.
4 days	Morula stage—special techniques can tell the sex of the new individual at this early stage.
7 to 9 days	Blastocyst stage—embryo reaches cavity of uterus and attaches to the lining of the uterine wall, burying itself in its glands.
2.5 to 4 weeks	Neurula stage—by three weeks the foundation for brain, spinal cord and entire nervous system are established. Blood vessels start forming at 2.5 weeks, the heart a day later. At 3.5 weeks, the heart, a simple tube, starts to pulsate. From three weeks, the primitive digestive system and the forerunner of the kidney form.
4.5 weeks	The 3 main parts of the brain are present. Eyes, ears, nasal organs, digestive tract, liver, gall bladder and arm and leg buds are forming.
5 weeks	Embryo is ⅓ inch long, and weighs 1/1000 oz. The early differentiation of the cerebral cortex is seen. Pituitary gland begins to form.

5.5 weeks   All muscle blocks present. Baby may begin to move, but mother does not feel this for another 6 to 10 weeks. The heart begins to subdivide into its 4 chambers.

6 weeks   Embryo is ½ inch long. Earliest reflexes can be elicited. Electrocardiogram (EKG) and electroencephalogram (EEG) can be recorded. Fingers, then toes, begin to form. Especially during the first 6 to 8 weeks of embryonic life, the embryo is most vulnerable to the effects of drugs, radiations, infections (particularly viral), noxious substances (such as alcohol and nicotine), and nutritional deficiencies of the mother.

8 weeks   Embryo is 1.5 inches long and weighs 1/30 oz. The face appears quite human. Heart completes the formation of its 4 chambers. Hands and feet are well-formed and distinctly human. Cerebral cortex begins to acquire typical cells. At the end of 8 weeks all organs, facial features and limb structures have begun to form. Everything is present that will be found in the new-born baby. The fundamental plan of the human body is completely mapped out by the end of the second month. During the remainder of pregnancy the various organs will mature in structure and function.

9 weeks   The growing child is now called a fetus. When the eyelids or palms of the hand are touched, they both respond by closing—this indicates that both nerves and muscles are functioning.

10 weeks   Except for refinements, the brain is much as it will be at birth. If the forehead is touched, the fetus turns the head away.

12 weeks
(3 months)   Fetus is 3 to 4 inches crown-rump length, and weighs about ½ oz. The thumb can now be opposed to the forefinger (a characteristic of all the primates). Fetuses of this age begin to show individual variations, probably based on behavioral patterns inherited from the parents. By the end of the 12th week, the fetus has developed all organ systems and is virtually a functioning organism. The fetal organs become more and more like what they will be in the newborn infant. Dr. Arnold Gessell, in his book *The Embryology of Behavior: The Beginnings of the Human Mind* has written: "And so, by the close of the first trimester, the fetus is a sentient, moving being. We need not pause to speculate as to the nature of his

	psychic attributes, but we may assert that the organization of his psychosomatic self is well under way."
4 months	Fingerprints, unique to the individual, are formed. The fetus responds to touch, and spontaneously stretches and exercises both arms and legs.
5 months	Fetus measures 8 inches crown-rump length, and weighs 8 to 10 oz. The fetus exhibits a firm hand grip, good muscular strength, coordination and reflex action, and kicks, moves, turns in the womb, hiccoughs, develops patterns of sleep and wakefulness, and reacts in an individual way to loud noise, or music or jarring or tapping the abdomen.
6 months	During this month, the eyes become sensitive to varying intensities of light and darkness but not to objects.
7 months	Fetus measures 12 inches crown-rump length and weighs 2 to 3 pounds. The fetus (now called a premature baby if born) continues growing and maturing. From the 7th to 9th month, every added day spent in the womb until birth prepares the baby all the better to assume an independent role.

Abortion and the Law

Here's another story as a way into our discussion. A friend of mine was visiting from France. On the way back from the airport to the Abbey my friend was amazed at my behavior. Each time we came to a red light I stopped even though there was no oncoming car with the right of way. Finally he said, "Why don't you drive on? It's so foolish to just sit. There is no car or police coming." At first I just chalked it up to cultural differences (though he seemed more pragmatic and impatient as a French-man than I did as an "up and doing" American). However, on deeper reflection this little incident highlighted Americans' overall respect for law and how deeply we prize a stable and just order. After all, wasn't it obvious that if everyone ran the light we would return to the Hobbesian world of "all against all"? Life can be "short, cruel, and brutish." No use adding to the chaos by running the light!

We Americans pride ourselves on being a "nation of laws rather than of men." The law protects, instructs and challenges us into becoming a community which holds certain things to be true and worthy of the highest sacrifices. To use the imagery of George F. Will, law is indispensable in the process of soul-making. There is for Americans a deep connection between the law and morality. At times we can uncritically conclude that what is declared legal or constitutional is moral. However, we know that at times our laws can be most immoral (slavery; denial of equal rights to women; denial of equal protection and due process to blacks and minorities; and the old Jim Crow laws to name but a few). Hence, we must be ever vigilant as to the moral quality of our laws and judicial decisions.

Because we so reverence the law and the Constitution we expect more from them than a neutral observer setting a contest between competing self-interests (the classical liberal view of the law as a watchman or referee which remains morally neutral and pushes religion into the private realm of heart, home and Sunday School). We want the law to reflect the highest ideals of our common covenant as a people. The laws we legislate and the Constitution we interpret should serve as beacons of "soul-making" and the formation of a "civic-self" which sacrifices for the common good. Issues arise which test the full measure of our laws, interpretations and ideals. Some issues are so fundamental that they reveal the basic values by which we live today and help shape tomorrow. One such issue is abortion.

In addition to issues which challenge and highlight our deepest held beliefs, there are issues which touch on many competing values at once. We find ourselves drawn in different directions as we try to be as wise as King Solomon. Abortion is one such issue which both reveals our deepest held beliefs and draws many competing values. The controversy and conflict seek resolution in a way that preserves the peace and respects the freedom of all citizens. More often than not in recent times we have turned to our courts for leadership and decision making. This is especially true of the Supreme Court of the United States.

Catholic theologian Christopher F. Mooney, S.J. in his book *Inequality and the American Conscience*, calls the Supreme Court the "National Conscience." Major cases (such as the *Bakke* case and affirmative action) often involve the claim of competing rights by individuals and individuals over against a certain class or group. Both parties have a legitimate rights claim. Both parties appeal to legal and Constitutional principles in order to legitimize their claim. How are we to settle such conflicts? We turn to the courts; especially the Supreme Court. Writing about the *Bakke* case Father Mooney holds:

> Resolving the *Bakke* conflict meant that the Court had to act in some sense as the nation's conscience . . . There must, then, be some choice by the nation of what our ideal of equality for the races means here and now . . . These are moral decisions, involving a choice of what is fair and just in society, for the "great fundamental guarantees of the Constitution are, after all, moral standards wrapped in legal comments" . . . the Supreme Court is forced to become in some sense the conscience of the nation, since its resulting opinion inevitably contributes to our general thinking about social justice.
>
> (*Inequality and the American Conscience*)

What Father Mooney writes about the Supreme Court and the *Bakke* case can be applied to the abortion issue. There are competing rights (the woman's right to privacy and reproductive sexual freedom in competition with the unborn's child's right to life) and the nation has looked to the Court for legal *and* moral guidance. The various abortion decisions from the Court have gone a long way in helping to shape the moral climate of the country. Many Americans believe that the Court has erred in its abortion decisions. The American conscience and "our general thinking about social justice" have been severely damaged (erroneously formed). Before we outline what can be done to correct the present legal situation, we need to examine the major recent abortion decisions by the Court. We shall limit our discussion to three major cases.

Roe v. Wade (1973). The Supreme Court on January 22, 1973 by a vote of 7-2 declared that the Texas abortion laws were unconstitutional. Pregnant women have a fundamental-constitutional *liberty* to an abortion. It is important that we *not* connect the *Wade* decision with abortion rights. For if we understand abortion as a constitutional right, then it could be legally required for those in the medical profession to provide the abortion. The outstanding Protestant *ethicist* Paul Ramsey of Princeton writes:

> There can be no more important point to make clear in the reader's, and in the public's mind than the fact that both Great Britain and the United States began with quite similar laws on the matter of abortion. In 1907 an act of Parliament and in 1973 the United States Supreme Court's decision *placed abortion in an area of liberties*. Neither nation established such a "right" to abortion that would entail an impelling duty on the part of members of the medical profession generally to provide such services or an obligation on the part of interns or nurses to participate in such procedures. (*Ethics at the Edge of Life*)

Professor Ramsey quotes Mr. Chief Justice Burger in support of the "clear and distinct" intention of abortion as a liberty and not a right: "Plainly, the Court today (the *Bolton* decision also in 1973) rejects any claim that the Constitution requires abortion on demand." However, as Professor Ramsey reminds us, it is a great naivete on the part of the Court not to believe that social pressure will be so great as to force conformity to abortion on demand. In fact this is precisely what has happened.

Further aspects of the *Roe v. Wade* decision declared that during the first trimester the liberty to an abortion cannot be interfered with by the state. The woman has unfettered freedom to such an abortion. However, in the *Wade-Bolton* decisions together, we witness a clear indication by the Court that the woman does not exercise her liberty in isolation from spouse and parents. The Court held that the pregnant woman is not "isolated in her privacy." As we shall see when we discuss the case of *Planned Parenthood* (1976) the woman does indeed become isolated and absolute in her privacy, her decision, and her "right" to an abortion. How this is done is worthy of George Orwell and Alice in Wonderland.

Roe v. Wade went on to indicate that the state can make its wishes felt after the first trimester only by acting on behalf of the mother's welfare. The unborn are not the concern. From viability to birth the state can act on behalf of the child *except* in those situations in which the mother's health is at stake. As one might expect, the meaning of "health" has been over-extended to such a degree that it has lost all value. Health becomes what the physician and/or woman decide it means. The full range of sicknesses, disturbances and inconveniences are included under the umbrella of health. While seeming to allow the state to speak on behalf of the voiceless unborn in the womb, it in reality allows abortion on demand by a judicial over-expansion of the concept "health."

Finally and most troubling of all, *Roe v. Wade* indicated that there was a general lack of agreement as to when human life began. Since there was no consensus by theologians, philosophers and scientists the Court stated it could not rule on such an issue. Such humility was short lived! For *Roe v. Wade* declared that the unborn child is not to be considered a person in the full Constitutional sense of the term. Therefore, the unborn child does not enjoy the basic rights of life, liberty, the pursuit of happiness and the Constitutional protections of the Fourteenth Amendment. What this means is simple: the Court does know and has determined to its satisfaction when human life begins and who is deserving of personhood in the full Constitutional sense of the term. Those inside the womb are not persons and those outside the womb are and must be granted full and equal protection under the law and Constitution.

Planned Parenthood (1976). This Court decision is sometimes referred to as the "Bicentennial Abortion Decision." It was released by the Supreme Court on July 1, 1976. Basically this decision declared unconstitutional two aspects of Missouri's anti-abortion laws. First, the Court declared unconstitutional the Missouri statute which required the father's consent for an abortion. Secondly, the Court ruled that it is unconstitutional to require the consent of a parent or guardian for an abortion on women who are unmarried or under the age of eighteen. The Supreme Court has in effect absolutized the decision concerning abortion to be that of the woman and hers alone. She need not consult any other person in making her private choice. In effect the Supreme Court has rendered the opinion that the woman's body is totally her own and the unborn child is part of that body. The husband and the family have no legal rights in the decision as to whether the unborn child will be aborted or allowed to live. Abortion is exclusively a woman's issue; men and family need not apply. And the Supreme Court concurs.

In our discussion of *Roe v. Wade* we made the careful distinction between a right and a liberty. We indicated that *Roe v. Wade* recognized the woman's liberty to have an abortion. We quoted Chief Justice Burger to the effect that there is no basis in the Constitution for abortion on demand. Furthermore, in the *Bolton* decision, the Court held that the abortion decision was not to be arrived at by the woman "isolated in her privacy." Yet we have just stated that the *Planned Parenthood* decision did exactly that—it placed the decision entirely in the hands of the woman free from any need to recognize the interests of father and family (the physician, however, still did not have to perform abortions against his conscience).

How did this reversal of so explicit a statement by the Chief Justice become reversed or amended in three short years? The judicial will can find a judicial way. The majority of the Court held that the spouse and family function as "agents of the state" and therefore their interference constitutes an unconstitutional interference with the woman's liberty (of course we mean absolute right!) to an abortion. The deeper level of shift between the rulings in *Wade* and *Bolton* and that of *Planned Parenthood v. Danforth* is really a shift in world views and fundamental assumptions about marriage and the role of society to make claims on our individualized rights and freedoms. The Missouri statute requiring the spouse's consent was grounded in the view of marriage as an institution which places limits on "absolute individualism." By contrast *Planned Parenthood* understands marriage to be a contract between consenting adults who *continue* to retain their individual rights. Abortion is the personal *right* of the woman over her own baby and reproductive system and she does not relinquish those rights when she marries. Husband and wife never become one flesh or reality. They never attain community. They remain nothing more than a bundle of individualized rights to be protected at all cost. Professor Ramsey says of the *Planned Parenthood* decision: "Seemingly gone from our law is any notion of the marriage bond or the state's long-standing interest in 'marriage as an institution.' In marriage today, the woman remains *la femme seule*. The husband remains *l'homme seul.*"

Parental consent fared no better than spouse consent. The Missouri statute required parental (or guardian) consent for an abortion during the first trimester unless a physician indicated the mother was in danger of death. The statute was based on the view of the state as protecting minors and helping parents discharge their duties. The Court ruled that this was unconstitutional because the State, like the spouse, cannot give what it does not properly own. Namely, the State cannot grant the right to veto a decision about abortion to the parents. In so doing we once again see the Court's view of family life and the role of children.

The *Planned Parenthood* decision by the Court revealed its liberal philosophical assumptions about the family. These assumptions cause the Court and our society as a whole to be both distrustful and antagonistic toward the family. Why? Because the family exists in opposition to everything political liberalism holds dear. The values of liberalism are a highly individualized notion of freedom and creativity; a very atomistic view of society and the individual; the idea that the basis of relationships are rational agreements based on self-interest; and the absence of loyalties or bonds that tie one to another. By contrast, the family is based on hierarchy, authority, tradition, bonding, community and a loyalty that makes blood thicker than self-interest. Professor Stanley Hauerwas captures the essence of this conflict:

> For family kinship has always been an anomaly for the liberal tradition. In liberal thought only if human beings can be separated in a substantial degree from kinship can they be free individuals subject to egalitarian policies of our society. Thus, for example, the Supreme Court recently held in *Planned Parenthood v. Danforth* that husbands have no rights if their wives wish an abortion, since "abortion is a purely personal right of the woman, and the status of marriage can place no limitation on person's rights." As Paul Ramsey has observed, in spite of our society's alleged interest in the bond of marriage, that bond is now under-

stood simply as a contract between individuals who remain as atomistic as before marriage.

(A Community of Character)

The Christian understands the family and the child in a vastly different light. The Second Vatican Council called the family "the little church." I take this to mean that the family is given the responsibility and grace to proclaim in word and deed the stories of Israel and Jesus about God's unbounded love, forgiveness, acceptance, peace and hope. The family becomes the first community for the child to be schooled in the ways of the Lordship of Jesus Christ. Rather than being private, isolated, atomized individuals, the family is a moral community which teaches that life is a gift to be received with gratitude and shared in humility. Children are not little adults who possess rights equal to their parents. Rather, they are gifts and signs of hope of what it means to live with care in a world this tragic and limited. Children are not atomized individuals locked in competition with parents, but opportunities to experience real love. Father James Tunstead Burtchaell, C.S.C., of Notre Dame University writes:

> Children are not threats to love or competitors for it—they are new claims upon it, new tugs on the ungenerous heart to force it open further than it felt it could go. Children don't divide parents' love; they invite it to multiply. Enormous resources of parent-love go stagnant in the heart's reservoirs for lack of children to make it gush and flow. Obviously, physical resources are not fathomless, and children must have bread. But in our age and culture, when parents feed their children cake and fear a shortage of bread, the church weeps—and rightly so—that the children are starving in a famine of love.
>
> ("What Children Teach Their Parents,"
> *Notre Dame Magazine.* Summer, 1984)

Beal v. Doe (1977). This decision by the Court has been viewed in some pro-life quarters as a victory for the rights of the unborn. The Court held that states are *not* required to use Medicaid money for non-therapeutic abortions. Some people have objected that this decision discriminates against the poor, holding that the poor woman is denied her "constitutional right" to an abortion. The rich have no problem securing their abortions. Those who advocate the state funding of abortions continue to speak about abortion as a "constitutional *right.*" Once again we must challenge this view. The Court ruled that abortion is a *liberty* which does *not* impose on the states or the medical profession the duty to see that the procedure is secured. However, it should be kept in mind that therapeutic abortions are still funded. Also, the definitions of what constitutes the therapeutic and non-therapeutic are as slippery as a greased pig. The understanding of *therapeutic,* like its cousin *health* in *Roe v. Wade* has been greatly over-extended. Perhaps the best we can say about *Beal* is that this decision clearly highlights the Court's confusion over abortion.

What are we to make of the Supreme Court decisions concerning abortion? Certainly we cannot go silently into that less than good night prepared by the "hierarchical magisterium" we call the Supreme Court. It is the responsibility of every citizen to question and analyze everything which comes from the majestic marble halls of our *judicial* government. Consider the wise words of Paul Ramsey: ". . . no hierarchical magisterium can function properly and wisely without vocal-if measured-dissent. Better decisions should come from those who, by office and calling, speak for us and for the Constitution as a living document that binds us together as a people." Ramsey goes even further in reminding us, and members of the Court, that "it is a civic duty" to question rulings. This is essential if a greater measure of reason is to be present. Otherwise the "Court would simply issue *rulings* if it did not intend its written *opinions* to be taken seriously."

The reaction of the American people as well as the legal community was strong and swift. This was especially true, as one might expect, concerning the *Roe v. Wade* decision. For this case served as the paradigm for subsequent rulings and reactions. Many legal scholars, whether they favor abortion or not, found the Court's decision in *Wade* most unsatisfactory. For example, Professor John Hart Ely of the Yale Law School said that *Wade* "is a very bad decision. It is bad because it is bad constitutional law, or rather because it is *not* constitutional law and gives almost no sense of an obligation to try to be." Former U.S. Solicitor General, and present Federal Court Judge (often mentioned as a prime candidate for the Supreme Court), Robert Bork said *Wade* is defective "because it is not grounded in law, only social policy."

Professor John T. Noonan, Jr. (see his outstanding book, *Private Choice*) has advanced the following criticism of the *Wade* decision: if the liberty to obtain an abortion is fundamental to the Constitution, why has it taken so long to articulate this liberty? Secondly, the Court has brought to American society abortion on demand. For the notion of "the mother's health" is so expansive that abortion will never be denied. Finally, the Court is guilty of using raw judicial power and of denying the democratic process. Constitutional government has been laid aside by a vote of "Seven Old Men." They have imposed their will on society as a whole. In effect, *Wade* is an excellent example of the Court passing and setting aside laws with no regard for constitutional government. The legislative and executive branches have been checked and the balance has shifted to the imperial judiciary.

The final voice is that of Professor Richard E. Morgan. In his excellent new book, *Disabling America: The "Rights Industry"* in

Our Time, Morgan terms the *Wade* decision, "an ill-considered judicial activism." Rather than win consensus and instruct the nation in law, *Wade* has brought about a division and agony that has grown through the years.

What can be done to move away from this legally troubling and morally tragic situation? Christians live by hope, and so we can hope that the Court will reverse itself. This is not unheard of. For example, the Supreme Court rejected the racially discriminatory notion of "separate but equal" held in *Plessy v. Ferguson* and ruled that this had no place in education with its landmark *Brown v. Board of Education*. However, changes in the Court through new thinking (a reading of newspapers) and new membership often takes time. Some have placed great hope in President Ronald Reagan's pro-life stance and the likelihood that he would be in a position to appoint as many as four new members of the Court. Once again this can be slow and not without problems of its own. There is no guarantee that a Supreme Court appointee will give relief in the area of abortion. Former President Dwight D. Eisenhower appointed what he thought to be a conservative to the Court. This "conservative" was Earl Warren!

In 1984 there were 1.5 million abortions performed in America. It would take a long time for the Court to rethink its position, as well as have new members appointed who are more sympathetic to the unborn. The unchecked destruction of human life demands a more immediate response. Other avenues of change must be tried. It is to the political process that we now turn our attention in hopes of protecting the unborn.

Political Action and Abortion

A number of significant strategies have been proposed as a way of changing and limiting the abortion environment in America. Some have called on Congress to employ its powers under Article III of the Constitution which allows it to exclude the Court from reviewing certain statutory or even constitutional issues. This would do more harm than good. Judicial review is a cherished part of our governmental tradition and a safeguard for individual freedom and protection. Abuses of judicial review are not arguments for its elimination. Professor Morgan, whom we quoted earlier, reminds us that what the Court "leaves behind is to be rejected, interpreted, applied and maintained until another majority forms to sweep the compact away or change it substantially."

A second approach, which is more appealing than the elimination of judicial review, calls for the passage of a constitutional amendment that would recognize the unborn child as a human person in the "full constitutional sense" of the term. This constitutional recognition of personhood would begin at the moment of conception and would extend to the child in the womb the same constitutional protections enjoyed by those outside the womb. There are a number of questions that arise with this approach.

America is a pluralistic society sprinkled with many religious, ethical and political views. There are many who would find a so-called "human life" amendment that places personhood at the moment of conception problematic. These Americans, opposed to abortion on demand and shocked by the present state of affairs, would want provisions that allow abortion in cases of rape, incest, and when the mother is in danger of death (some would want to include cases of fetuses with severe genetic defects). At the other end of the spectrum are Americans who want a "human life" amendment that outlaws *all* abortion save in the case of saving the life of the mother, certified by a licensed physician. At present the pro-life movement is a house divided on the very substance of the amendment. Such a division cannot long be tolerated if there is to be any reasonable hope of passing such an amendment.

What could be done to unify the various pro-life groups? Without sacrificing our principles and belief in the sacredness of all life, it seems that given the present moral climate we should join forces in order to work for an amendment that would limit abortions to cases of rape, incest, and when the life of the mother is at stake. This type of moral compromise (St. Alphonsus Liguori) in no way calls a halt to our efforts (over the long haul) to secure an amendment which would restrict abortion even further. However, *in the short run* something must be done that is feasible in the Thomistic sense of the term, that is, a law that is capable of being reasonably enforced and one that does not bring the law into disrespect by promising or expecting too much.

Some of the Catholic community's most respected voices have advanced such a compromise. For example, Father Theodore M. Hesburgh, C.S.C., President of Notre Dame University, has written in *Catholicism in Crisis*:

> Generally the pro-life movement has been for an absolute prohibition of abortion. If such a total solution is not possible in our pluralistic society, and, in fact, was voted down by national referendum in Catholic Italy, will Catholics cooperate with other Americans of good will and ethical conviction to work for a more restrictive abortion law? One might hope so. This would not compromise our belief in the sanctity of all human life. We should continue to hold ourselves to a higher standard than we can persuade society-at-large to write into laws.

The noted Catholic priest and philosopher Joseph F. Donceel, S.J. has written an article in *America* ("Catholic Politicians and Abortion," Feb. 2, 1985) in which he advocates a unique collaboration between pro-life and pro-choice politicians who find abortion on demand troubling. How is this to be done? In the words of Father Donceel:

Might not both pro-lifers and pro-choicers be willing to make some concessions in order to reach some agreement? The Catholic pro-lifers would admit that for those who do not take as a guideline the teachings of the Catholic Church—more specifically, who reject both the theory of instant humanization and of anticipated homicide—abortion during early pregnancy is not murder and might be allowed when serious reasons call for it. And the Catholic pro-choice politician, keeping in mind these restrictions (during early pregnancy, for serious reasons) would promise to help curb abortion on demand. Thus both parties would move in the direction of the position that, according to the public opinion polls, the majority of the American people (who are aware that eggs are not chickens) seem to adopt.

A third approach to tempering abortion on demand is advanced by Father Richard A. McCormick, S.J. He advocates working through state legislatures in a democratic way to bring about change. This approach is certainly preferable to the shabby, inadequate and undemocratic work of the Supreme Court. The Christian has a responsibility to labor on behalf of justice and respect for human life. The Christian must resist the temptation to withdraw from the public debate. In fact, we must keep the debate going lest we forget what is at stake for all of us. What we Christians are doing, slowly and often in unspectacular ways, is effecting a revolution of conscience and consciousness.

We are working to correct the vision of our society (William F. May) and inviting all to hear the cries of the poor man Lazarus who now resides in the unborn. Christian theologian Gilbert Meilaender ("Euthanasia & Christian Vision," *Thought* Vol. 57. December, 1982) indicates that moral reflection is not primarily about guilt, responsibility and punishment. Rather, our moral reflection "is, first and foremost, one of the ways in which we train ourselves and others to see the world rightly." Along with the blind man in the Gospel we need to see the world rightly and have our vision corrected. This is especially true for a society that values trees, swamps and the life of a baboon more than the unborn. No law can fully provide this correction. Only collective conversion of heart will allow us to see that in the presence of each human being we stand on sacred ground.

Our reflections on political action and abortion will conclude with some very wise thoughts by Father Daniel A. Degnan, S.J., a teacher in the law school of Seton Hall University. Father Degnan invites us to consider what we ought to *prudently* expect from ourselves and our *political leaders* who oppose abortion (see "Prudence, Politics and the Abortion Issue," *America*. Feb. 16, 1985). He defines prudence in the following way: "Prudence in the classical sense concerns judgments about action. Prudence describes effective, wisely chosen action for the sake of an end or goal. Prudence is right action, not caution." How does this understanding of prudence translate into political action concerning abortion?

Father Degnan advocates the passage of a constitutional amendment restricting abortions or at least an amendment which would return the debate to the *state* legislatures (similar to Father McCormick). Secondly, Degnan holds that "in the highest sense, the protection of human rights, is the first responsibility of political leaders." Unfortunately our political leaders have not done this in the case of the unborn (most seek a "safe" position by embracing the private choice view of the Supreme Court). Such politicians must render an account of their stewardship before the electorate.

Does Father Degnan fall victim to the so-called "one issue" politics that the pro-lifers are often accused of? Human life issues are of the highest order. Hence, abortion is one issue that grabs our attention in more than a passing way. However, Degnan attaches three prudential principles in order to avoid a kind of reflex replacement of political leaders. First, we cannot expect our political leaders to do the impossible. We must realistically evaluate the political climate. Second, we need not try to accomplish everything at once in only one way. One generation sows; another reaps. Yet we must continue to work for that time when all human life is respected and accorded full rights. Degnan's final principle is the most important, namely, that political leaders must work for the common good. This working for the common good concerning abortion is especially acute for those in Congress and the State legislatures. Why? Because the President or governor is pressed on every side by a host of issues which demand immediate action. They can offer the leadership of encouragement, but the "leg work" must be done by elected state and federal political office-holders.

A brief postscript to this section on political action and abortion seems called for. As I am writing these words a new controversy is raging concerning abortion and the debate process. Various pro-life groups have just released (February 12, 1985) a very explicit film about abortion entitled, *The Silent Scream* (this film is narrated by Dr. Bernard N. Nathanson, once director of the largest abortion clinic in the Western world). Dr. Nathanson has become one of the most forceful spokesmen for the pro-life movement. Why? He became "deeply troubled by [his] own increasing certainty that [he] had in fact presided over 60,000 deaths." Many in the pro-choice group (for example Ms. Judy Goldsmith, President of N.O.W.) have screamed (pardon the expression) "foul." Why? Because pro-choicers believe that this is nothing but a low-level appeal to emotionalism and sentimentality.

The film has been sent to each member of the full Congress (the White House has played a part in the distribution) and has been shown on national cable television. The film is powerful and graphic. It shows the actual abortion of a twelve-week-old (there is some debate about the exact age) unborn child through the S & C method (this procedure is discussed in our earlier section on the medical aspects of abortion). There is a freeze-frame in which the unborn turns to the viewer and opens its mouth as if it is crying out for help. There is none. Pro-choicers have indicated that they want the scream of the unborn to remain silent as well as invisible.

Yet there are situations which we must keep ever before our eyes lest we forget. We need to see the demonic of the Third Reich. The death camps must serve as perpetual reminders of just how absolute the corruption of power can be. So it is with abortion. We must remove "the vale of ignorance" so prized by today's liberated, comfortable and utilitarian society. Abortion is not the "delivery" of a dead baby but the killing of a human being. We cannot remain blissfully ignorant of what an abortion is. For while the scream of the unborn may be silent to us (this silence itself is a sad commentary on our condition) it reaches the ears of the One in whose image we are *all* wonderfully made.

Abortion and Morality

Ultimately it is not the wonders of modern medicine or the majesty of law that the Christian brings to the abortion debate. We bring our stories of God revealed through Israel and Jesus, along with our community reflections on what it means to be an *imago Dei*. The Christian brings to the public square a wisdom the world deems foolishness and a strength that seems weak. We bring a faith which seeks justice through reverencing all human life. Let us briefly examine the biblical narrative and the Catholic tradition which helps to form the kind of people we are and the way in which we value (or better envision) human life.

The temptation is strong (and one certainly not resisted by those who try to win the politics of abortion by appealing to repressed anti-Catholic feelings) to understand abortion as "the

Catholic issue." Hence, it becomes crucial for us to insist from the beginning that the faith we proclaim and voice on behalf of the unborn finds deep roots in the God of Abraham, Isaac, Jacob, Jesus, Luther, Barth, Paul VI and John Paul II. The stories of our biblical faith proclaim the following about human life: it is a gift and trust from the God who creates, redeems and transforms that life into a new creation. Human life is not just one creation among other moments of creation. Human life is a unique, sacred moment when God breathes into the day with the Divine breath. Man became alive with the very spirit of God. Human life is a gift entrusted to us which deserves the highest respect. The respect we extend to human life is ultimately the respect and acknowledgment we give to God. By respecting the alien dignity of each person we proclaim the Lordship of the God of Life.

The great Protestant theologian Karl Barth understood the Lordship of Jesus Christ as extending throughout the universe and into the womb. Barth writes:

> This child is a man for whose life the Son of God has died, for whose unavoidable part in the guilt of all humanity and future individual guilt He has already paid the price. The true light of the world shines already in the darkness of the mother's womb. And yet they want to kill him deliberately because certain reasons which have nothing to do with the child himself favor the view that he had better not be born! Is there any emergency which can justify this? It must surely be clear to us that until the question is put in all its gravity a *serious* discussion of the problem cannot even begin, let alone lead to serious results.
>
> (*Church Dogmatics*. III/4)

Professor Barth is reminding us of the central vision of the biblical story: God is the One who is in control of all reality. God alone is sovereign and we are called to surrender in trust to the One who is faithful to the end, and to a new beginning. Man need not come to God with all his achievements, technology and economic clout. Such boasting only serves to mask our true need. We can come to God in all of our poverty knowing that we shall never be turned away empty.

The biblical narrative that proclaims God's unbounded love for us does not stop there. Those who profess Jesus as Lord are called and empowered to love as He loved. That is, Jesus loved those who found themselves outside the parameters of everyone's love. Jesus accepted those who daily knew rejection and isolation. Love made the leper clean. Love forgave sins and challenged the lame to walk and the blind to see. Jesus did not pick and choose whom He would love. He loved all persons and invited them to new life. Professor Stanley Hauerwas writes:

> It is the Christian belief, nurtured by the command of Jesus, that we must learn to love one another, that we become more nearly what we were meant to be through the recognition and love of those we did not "choose" to love. Children, the weak, the ill, the dispossessed provide a particularly intense occasion for such love, as they are beings we cannot control. We must love them for what they are rather than what we want or wish them to be, and as a result we discover that we are capable of love.
>
> (*A Community of Character*)

Such a love has about it a universal quality which moves it beyond the limits of the Christian community. To love the unlovable and the defenseless could serve to unite all men and women of good will into a world family that "speaks for the children."

The biblical vision and story of respect and love for all human life is a foundational aspect of the Catholic moral tradition. The number of documents and statements by the hierarchical magisterium on this subject is enormous. A clear statement of the Church's position is contained in *Humanae Vitae* by Pope Paul VI: "Directly willed and procured abortion, even if for therapeutic reasons, is always condemned." Catholic bioethicist Father Richard A. McCormick, S.J. has provided a great service to the Church through his many years of summarizing and analyzing various ethical issues. In his book, *How Brave A New World?* he has listed eight common themes of the official Church teaching:

1. The right to life is one that is present from the moment of conception. The Church has gone on record as defending human life at its earliest edge—conception. For example, the *Pastoral Constitution on the Church in the Modern World* declares: "Life must be protected with utmost care from the moment of conception: abortion and infanticide are abominable crimes." The Vatican Congregation for the Doctrine of the Faith issued a *Declaration on Abortion*, which teaches: "The tradition of the Church has always held that human life must be protected and favored from the beginning . . . In the *Didache* (90 A.D.) it is clearly stated: 'You shall not kill by abortion . . . You shall not murder the infant already born.' " These two examples are important in light of the recent controversy concerning a pluralism of Catholic views on abortion and the need for dialogue. While there may be individual Catholics, or groups of Catholics, who have held different views about the morality of abortion, the magisterial teaching has been consistent. Direct abortion cannot be morally justified. It is a direct attack on innocent life.

2. The right to life is a fundamental value that is essential to social justice and the welfare of the community as a whole.

3. It is the duty of civil society to protect human life in *all* its forms.

4. Human life is a continuum from the beginning. From the moment of conception we have a human person in the process of becoming.

5. Abortion will weaken the bonds of society and usher in personal and social evils. Christians and people of good will must work to eliminate the causes of abortion.

6. The respect for nascent life must be done in light of the various cultures and legal traditions of a given society.

7. The magisterial teaching on abortion extends beyond the Roman Catholic community and is addressed to *all* people of good will.

I believe that direct abortion is an unjustified attack on innocent human life. I am uneasy with the language of "proportionate reason" and "quality of life." If all people had the faith and compassion of Father McCormick, I could be won over. However, in a society which is so comfort-oriented and utilitarian I fear the great abuses that have and will occur. I believe that the Catholic Church stands in a very prophetic way for life in a world that knows so much death; that it is a Church of peace in a world that courts violence. In the words of Pope John Paul II from his October 7, 1979 talks delivered at the Capitol Mall in Washington, D.C.:

> I do not hesitate to proclaim before you and before the world that all human life—from the moment of conception and through all subsequent stages—is sacred, because human life is created in the image and likeness of God . . . And so we stand up every time that human life is threatened. — When the sacredness of life before birth is attacked, we will stand up and proclaim that no one ever has the authority to destroy unborn life.   ("Stand Up for Human Life")

Pastoral Care and Abortion

In his book, *Critical Concerns in Moral Theology*, Father Charles E. Curran, professor of moral theology at the Catholic University of America has written: "Catholic moral theology has always been intimately connected with pastoral practice. Moral theology exists primarily in and for the Church and serves the life of the community of believers . . . The entire history of moral theology has been very much influenced by pastoral practice." This insightful reminder by Father Curran helps us to keep ever before our eyes the primacy of persons on the journey toward God. Moral theology has shifted enormously since the early 1960's. The doing of moral theology has shifted from one using manuals for the training of confessors to one in which we hope to move toward a deeper relationship with Christ. None of this is said as a rejection of the intellectual and philosophical aspects of our theology. Moral theology today aims at connecting the head *and* heart. Holiness is wholeness.

Moral theology is part of the ongoing life of the community of believers and is used to help promote life in abundance. However, we live in a world that is sinful and broken. We live in need of healing. Many Catholics are separated from their faith community because of divorce and remarriage, the inability to deal with change, and yes—abortion. An essential part of a pastoral moral theology demands that we creatively and lovingly deal with those who are broken. We will have to take risks like the Forgiving Father in Luke's Gospel who burst from the porch at the sight of his child who was lost and given up for dead. Part of resurrection is coming home in order to be re-established as son or daughter. Many Catholics need to be embraced; have the ring put on their finger; and have the fatted calf killed so the celebration can begin. Why? Because the lost have been found and the dead have come to life. As heaven rejoices, so must the community of faith on earth rejoice in obedience to God's joyful will.

If our moral theology concerning abortion is also to be one of prudent pastoral practice, the following should be kept in mind:

1. The Catholic Church must continue to prophetically witness to the sacredness of all human life from womb to tomb. This teaching cannot be compromised. There is only one ultimate Lord of Love—Jesus Christ. We are *not* being compassionate when we fail to tell people the truth that will set them free. At the same time we need to make sure that our teaching is motivated by love in imitation of Jesus, the Divine Teacher. True teaching is never vindictive or punishing. It seeks to liberate the mind and heart so as to respond to God and neighbor. We must make sure that our teaching on abortion avoids the admonition of Father John Catoir, director of the Christophers: "It is possible to crush the human spirit by an attitude that appears to lack compassion. Our documents may be intended to straighten people out, but they very often drive people away" (see Catoir's article "Is the Church Unforgiving?" in *America*, January 19, 1985).

2. Of the 1.5 million abortions in America in 1984, a good number of the women were Catholics. They challenge our ability to heal and reconcile. We cannot leave the impression that these women have committed the ultimate sin for which there is no forgiveness. To do so would simply compound the tragedy of abortion: the death in the womb would be matched by the spiritual death of despair. Guilt is an enormous burden. It calls for enormous healing and the forgiving power of Jesus. In no way does this mean that we are going "soft on abortion." Rather, we are following the example of Jesus and the insight of St. Thomas Aquinas: justice without mercy is

cruelty. Again, the wise words of Father Catoir: "Embracing the sinner is not a sign of laxity. It is not a matter of compromise. We cannot give moral permission to sinners, but we can try to understand their pain . . . It is not enough for us to chastise and correct sinners. We must love them . . . If we do not make an effort to encourage the weak, our theological correctness becomes moral arrogance."

3. The Catholic Church has, in my opinion, begun to accept the challenge of being a prophetic voice for life, theologically sound on life issues and pastorally sensitive to the pain of those who have had abortions. The witness of many bishops and Church leaders at the diocesan and parish levels, have indicated a refusal to be satisfied with the teaching that does not find completion in action. Church leaders have become increasingly sensitive to the needs of women who find themselves with an unwanted pregnancy. The Church has begun to say, "You may not want this child, but we do. And we will do all in our power to help you make a decision that will witness for life." I cite merely one example, though for me it is a most profound one, of a moral theology that is pastorally prudent.

Archbishop John J. O'Connor of New York delivered an address ("Human Lives, Human Rights," October 15, 1984) at Cathedral High School in which he expressed his understanding of women who find themselves frantic about a pregnancy they don't want. Rather than condemn such women, Archbishop O'Connor said, "I would do anything I could to help them pick up the pieces of their lives after an abortion." But what about the Church's response to women who have not yet had an abortion but feel trapped? Archbishop O'Connor has made an unequivocal commitment of the Archdiocese to "every single or married woman facing an unplanned pregnancy, that the Archdiocese of New York will give you free, confidential help of highest quality . . . The Archdiocese of New York is prepared to do everything in its power to help you and your unborn baby, to make absolutely certain that you never need feel that you must have an abortion." This commitment is extended to every woman regardless of race, creed or color. Services include medical care, social work, living arrangements during pregnancy, financial aid and spiritual support for those who keep their babies, and adoption for those who feel they cannot meet the ongoing demands of motherhood. All of this is done with absolute confidentiality. The actions of Archbishop O'Connor, and many like him, fulfill the challenge of the Epistle of James: "You see that faith was active along with his works, and faith was completed by works" (Jm 2:22).

4. Violence begets violence. Recently we have witnessed a number of bombings of abortion clinics by so-called "pro-life advocates." In the name of respecting life and valuing the unborn, buildings are destroyed with the moral legitimation that "this is God's will." Hardly. Taking up the sword (or the TNT) was ruled out of order by the One who went to Golgotha in order to bring a peace that the world cannot give or understand. The churches and pro-life groups must state clearly that such violence is unacceptable. Some means cannot be used to achieve our goals no matter how praiseworthy the latter are. The means must be moral as well as the end. But beyond all this, the Christian community is called to dwell in the world of violence as a community of peace. Father David B. Burrell, C.S.C. of Notre Dame University has written: "So the primary task of those who would make Jesus' story theirs is to stand within that world—their world— witnessing to a peaceable Kingdom which reflects the

right understanding of that very world." The abortion laws (or lack thereof) must be changed. However, we must work within the democratic process. This no doubt will be slow. However, as people of "the peaceable Kingdom" we must be schooled in patience and hope.

5. A final pastoral consideration is directed to those who work in the professions of medicine and law. The churches and temples have an important mission to work and witness for life in partnership with our brothers and sisters who labor in hospitals and courts. The respect for life is not limited to the church and synagogue. The highest ideals of medicine (the Hippocratic Oath) and law (the Constitution and inalienable rights) converge with the ideals and values of the world's great religions. Abortion is offering us a splendid opportunity to form a covenant for life. In so doing we can help realize the vision of Senator Hubert Humphrey: "The moral test of government is how it treats those who are in the dawn of life—the children; those who are in the twilight of life—the aged; and those who are in the shadows of life—the sick, the needy and handicapped."

Conclusion and Transition

We have come a long way in our reflections, yet the frustration remains that there are still "miles to go" before the unborn are cherished as gift and hope. In these pages I have attempted to outline the issues, analyze the arguments fairly, treat all with respect, and prudently suggest ways to authentically witness to life. No attempts have been made to hug the middle course so as to avoid the exposure of my own convictions. I believe abortion is wrong. It is a direct attack on innocent, defenseless human life. I believe that abortion is an ultimate rejection of the Lordship of

Jesus Christ. At the same time, I feel compassion for women who find themselves with an unwanted pregnancy. I feel hopeful that the Catholic Church (along with many others) is moving to pastorally respond to such situations with a faith that is loving and healing.

The title of this chapter is a take-off from the well-known poem *Meditation XVIII* by John Donne. I have phrased it in the form of a question. The tolling bell carries a message. It can toll the message of death or it can ring out with the joy of life and hope. In other words, its ringing can herald the good news that *all* human beings are honored and welcomed in our world because of who they are and what they mean for the world to come. A great deal will depend on our actions and commitment to life. As Donne reminds us: every passing of a fellow human being makes us less than we were before. This sense of solidarity with life, with all life, is crucial for society. Jean Rostand has written:

> Yes, I admit that I would be repelled and saddened if I witnessed the development of a social ethic in which the value of every life ceased to be infinite . . . I have the weakness to believe that it is an honor for a society to desire the expensive luxury of sustaining life for its useless, incompetent and incurably ill members; I would almost measure a society's degree of civilization by the amount of effort and vigilance it imposes on itself out of pure respect for life. It is noble to struggle unrelentingly to save someone's life, as if he were dear to us, when objectively he has no value and is not even loved by anyone.
>
> (*Humanly Possible: A Biologist's Notes on the Future of Mankind*)

What Dr. Rostand says about the unwanted outside the womb certainly applies to those inside the womb.

The closing of this chapter with the words of Rostand is not accidental. For the threat to human life is not limited to the unborn. This threat becomes extended to the "other edge of life" and to all points in between. We attack the unborn because they are not wanted or their life would be a burden (to *them*, of course!). The same logic and rationalization is easily extended to the defective newborn, the sick and dying, and the elderly who have used up their allotted days and are "not even loved by anyone."

In our next chapter we shall extend our defense of life to those who have made it through the womb, but now find themselves under attack. And so, for whom does the bell toll? For all of us. What will its tolling signify?

III

Euthanasia:
The Right To Die . . . The DUTY To Die?

Whose Life Is It?

Our intellectual ancestors, the Greek philosophers, were fond of using dialogue and conversation as a way of discovering one's beliefs, the limits of those beliefs, and the possibility of changing them. In other words, conversation has the potential for being more than "idle talk." There is something dramatic and revealing about the exchange of words and ideas. A recent conversation I had with a friend while watching an interview program occasioned the sharing of beliefs about human life, the taking of life, and what it means to care for and cherish our loved ones. Needless to say, the conversation proved to be quite dramatic.

The interview program dealt with the topic of euthanasia and the right to die with dignity. The gentleman being interviewed advocated euthanasia and had killed his wife who was dying of cancer. Because this act of euthanasia was done in a country which legally tolerates such behavior, he was on television and not in jail. Furthermore, he had just written a book which not only advocated euthanasia but was the first detailed "how to" book on the subject. While this man spoke I couldn't help but be taken back by his calm, matter-of-fact approach.

Running through my mind was the thought, "This guy has just told a national audience that he killed his wife. Granted the motive was 'mercy,' but how can he be so analytical?" The longer the interview went on, the more uncomfortable I became.

I turned to my friend and voiced not only my uneasiness with this man's attitude but also that I was in moral disagreement with his advocacy of euthanasia. To my surprise he said, "I thought he made a great deal of sense. I think he did the right thing." At this point I wasn't sure which I felt more—surprise at the euthanasia advocate on television or the advocate next to me.

I said to my friend, "Bob, this man just admitted killing his wife. Doesn't that shock you?" "Not at all," said Bob, "the man was acting out of a sense of compassion. His wife didn't know what was going to happen. He was simply trying to relieve her of suffering. I think he was a good husband. Can't you imagine the pain he felt?"

"Bob," I said, "how can you talk about compassion and his pain? What about the wife? I don't think we can take the life of another in the name of compassion, care or love. How do we know she wanted to die? Maybe she would have recovered. Physicians are not infallible with their prognosis."

We went back and forth for some time. Finally, Bob said, "Look Bill, the issue ultimately comes down to the question, 'Whose life is it anyway?' We have to make these difficult decisions. We live in a complex world. Part of being free and mature is doing what that husband did. He is the courageous modern man."

As Bob spoke his piece I could not help but think of the words of Max Stirner (1806-1856): "All truths that are *beneath* me are dear to me, but I do not acknowledge any truth *above* me, any truth I would have to take as guide. For me there is no truth because there is nothing superior to me! Neither my own essence nor the essence of man as such is superior to me!" What my friend Bob, Stirner, Nietzsche and many today hold as absolute truth is this: each individual must make his own rules and values. Each person is a law unto himself. The individual, private self is the highest court at which we stand in judgment. Each individual is free to do as he pleases. Freedom is a life without limits or a superior authority. Ultimate freedom is expressed in the act of pure willing. The goals do not matter. What is of utmost importance is merely that one wills with all of one's might.

Yet is this authentic freedom? Is this not in reality a deeper, though often unrecognized, movement into slavery? One becomes the slave of the unschooled, limitless ego which always demands more (money, power, success or any countless number of idols). The essential misconception (or illusion) of such a view of freedom is the belief that the individual is the source of life and meaning. What is not properly seen is our true condition as human beings. We are finite, contingent and needful. The brokenness and limitations of the human condition cannot be overcome by boasting or grasping. In fact, it is the very attitude of boasting and the act of grasping that ushered in our fallen human condition.

The Christian story understands freedom in a vastly different manner. For the Christian, freedom is a mature, responsive self-surrender to God in an act of loving trust. Authentic freedom is the risk of letting go all that promises us life in the here and now and relying on the Word who became flesh. True liberty comes to the one who is willing to allow God's story to be told through the story of his personal life. This understanding of freedom is powerfully captured by Father René Latourelle, S.J.:

> Christians who realize that the meaning of their existence and activity can develop fully only in Jesus Christ, will, like Christ, adopt a filial manner of life. They orient their freedom in terms of *vocation* and the *following of Christ*. The certainty that they have received from Christ an unambiguous Gift, namely, the Spirit of love who liberates us from

our self-centeredness in all its forms, makes it possible for them to be fully free. Their responsible autonomy is not taken away, but it is exercised in the light of a revelation regarding the deepest meaning of life, namely, that they are set free from their sinful condition and are called to the life of the Spirit. Their activity is guided by the Spirit of love; and because they love what is asked of them, they are not subject to the constraints of the law. Or more accurately, love itself is the law.

(*Man and His Problems in the Light of Jesus Christ*)

If we fail to so understand what authentic freedom is about, the result is self-centeredness and the will-to-power. Anything or anyone standing in the way of "my freedom" must be destroyed. In the words of Stanley Hauerwas: "Violence results from our attempting to live our lives without recognizing our falsehoods. Violence derives from the self-deceptive story that we are in control—that we are our own creators—and that only we can bestow meaning on our lives, since there is no one else to do so" (*The Peaceable Kingdom*).

Bob's question "Whose life is it?" is crucial. His understanding of freedom moves him to respond that each individual is the private owner of his or her life. Hence, Bob could find nothing morally objectionable (in fact it was a badge of courage and maturity) with the taking of this woman's life by her husband. After all, his will was the will-to-compassion. It just so happened that in this instance compassion called for the direct killing of an innocent human being. By contrast, the Christian story proclaims a freedom that recognizes (and rejoices in) a responsibility to a Reality higher than the self. It acknowledges a Giver of life for whom we must render an account of our stewardship. The narrative about God which structures our freedom and the ways we treat one another simply forbids the direct killing of an innocent brother and sister. Life is a gift which is not subject to cancellation on the basis of our merely willing it so. Helmut Thielicke writes: "Because of this alien dignity, the shell that remains is not under our control. Actively killing it off is a crime; it violates what is inviolable." (*Being Human . . . Becoming Human*).

After my conversation with Bob I wondered how many people believe that euthanasia is morally permissible. To my surprise, I found that many today hold acceptable some form of euthanasia. This prompted me to search for some statistics by which to judge the national mood. I'm not saying that moral decisions are to be decided by a poll or a show of hands. Democracy does not settle morality. However, if we believe that the wish is the father of thought which fathers the deed, then it does matter a great deal what people think at a given time.

Professor William J. Monahan, Associate Professor of Sociology at St. Louis University, has written an article entitled, "Contemporary American Opinion on Euthanasia" (see the excellent *Moral Responsibility In Prolonging Life Decisions*, Pope John XXIII Center, which contains the article). Dr. Monahan's research is based on various polls concerned with the euthanasia issue from 1936 through 1978. While there are no statistics available through 1986, a very clear picture emerges: at least 50% of the population supports the idea of direct euthanasia. At least 66% favor a withdrawal of life-support systems from the terminally ill. On the positive side, almost 75% of those polled answered "no" to the following question: "Do you think a person has the moral right to end his or her life when this person is an extremely heavy burden on his or her family?" Professor Monahan concludes, "This suggests an affirmation of family relationships in the face of serious illness. The invocation of family ties seems to elicit a sense of support and a choice of life, rather than being a reason for ending life." However, the overall picture that emerges from this study leaves us with a less than hopeful analysis: ". . . a steadily increasing proportion of Americans, now well over half, favor euthanasia. Such widespread support, if only at the level of opinions, creates an ambiance in which more determined effort must be made to apply Christian criteria in making decisions to prolong life."

What follows is a determined effort to take up the challenge of Professor Monahan and apply Catholic-Christian criteria (though I would certainly not want to exclude the other great religions or all people of good will) for the making of decisions that respect life. In this chapter we shall explore the basic concepts used in the euthanasia debate, which will provide a common terminology for discussion. We shall then examine the magisterial teaching on euthanasia. Special attention will be given to the excellent document on euthanasia (1980) released by the Sacred Congregation for the Doctrine of the Faith. Then we shall examine some of the leading theological reflections on euthanasia and briefly consider the legal status on euthanasia in our society. Of particular importance is the issue of neonatal care, especially concerning the proper care of children who are born with severe handicaps and genetic defects. Besides examining the difficult ethical questions that arise, we shall offer a meditation on the proper way to reverence "the little ones" who come to us with special needs. Finally, we shall close with a reflection on the mystery of human suffering and what the Christian story holds for us as a proper response.

Conceptual Landscape

What is euthanasia? The word itself comes from the Greek and means "good death" or "dying well." The moral strain comes when we begin to flush out what is meant by "good" and "well." Slogans are a seductive misuse of language. They leave the impression that a great deal has been said when in fact more has been hidden or confused. Hence, we hear such expressions as "death with dignity" and "dying one's own death humanly."

What do these expressions mean? In the modern context such talk is usually associated with the removal of various life sustaining procedures when they do not sustain life but prolong dying. However, as Paul Ramsey reminds us, there is no real dignity to dying and death. Death is a shock and affront to human dignity. The removal of various machines and tubes does not lessen the indignity. The real dignity present in such situations is the faithful, total commitment to the dying person. As Ramsey is fond of saying, there are limits to our curing but never to our caring. Needless to say, there has been much confusion surrounding the discussion of euthanasia or "the good death." This confusion yields serious consequences.

The discussion of euthanasia calls for us to make some careful conceptual distinctions. We can distinguish four (4) careful classifications of euthanasia:

1. *Voluntary euthanasia.* An act whereby the patient is killed through his or her free consent.

2. *Involuntary euthanasia.* An act whereby the patient is killed without his or her knowledge or consent.

3. *Direct (positive-active) euthanasia.* A willful action which brings about the death of another. Direct euthanasia can be realized in a number of ways: an overdose of pills, improper usage of medications, lethal injection, and a number of more violent ways (such as the use of a gun).

4. *Indirect (negative-passive) euthanasia.* The willful omission of treatment necessary for the sustaining of only biological life.

It is crucial to keep these categories in mind. Throughout our discussion on euthanasia we must make a clear moral distinction between *direct killing* and *letting die.* This distinction is essential in answering the question: Is there any *moral* difference between the willful, direct taking of another's life and allowing one to die one's own death by refraining from acting? The answer comes down to one of ethical methodology. From the perspective of *moral consequentialism* the answer is "no." The consequentialist holds that in both cases, direct action and allowing to die, the result is the same—the person dies. Hence, since the results or consequences are the same so is the moral outcome. If it is morally permissible to let someone die because further treatment would be useless or extraordinary, then it is morally permissible to directly act so as to hasten their death. The *means* are not of primary moral concern.

However, the consequentialist position has been challenged on a number of fronts (not just by the magisterial teaching of the Catholic Church). For example, moral philosopher Charles Fried in his book, *Right and Wrong*, makes the distinction between actions of purpose and actions of routine. Professor Fried is reminding us that we cannot lose sight of our *intentions* in a given situation. Though our different actions may produce the same results, this in no way means that the actions are morally the same. Gilbert Meilaender, Assistant Professor of Religion at Oberlin College, makes use of Fried's distinction in terms of aim and result. He writes:

> This distinction between aim and result is also helpful in explaining the moral difference between euthanatizing a suffering person near death and simply letting such a person die. Suppose this patient were to stop breathing, we were to reject the possibility of resuscitation, and then the person were suddenly to begin breathing again. Would we, simply because we had been willing to let this patient die, now proceed to smother him so that he would indeed die? Hardly. And the fact that we would not indicates that we did not *aim* at his death (in rejecting resuscitation), though his death could have been one *result* of what we did aim at (namely, proper care for him in his dying). By contrast, if we euthanatized such a person by giving him a lethal injection, we would indeed aim at his death; we would

invest the act of aiming at his death with personal involvement of our purpose.   ("Euthanasia & Christian Vision,"
Thought Vol. 57, No. 227. December, 1982)

The consequentialist position has grown in popularity in recent times. There are a number of reasons for this. Euthanasia is often presented as a humane, compassionate response on the part of the patient or another in order to relieve excessive suffering through death. However, the Christian story does not allow us to understand love, compassion, care and humane treatment in such terms. Our narrative does not make room for the direct killing of the innocent regardless of the values which plead its case. The Christian story invites us to transcend the "natural" and move into the realm of God's covenantal care. Such a movement challenges us to trust that the One who authors all life is at the same time the One who redeems, heals, and brings all life to its blessed perfection in him.

A second reason that consequentialism is attractive is found in the praiseworthy desire to correct the ills of the individual and society. We moderns (and this is especially true of the American variety) like to believe that there is no task beyond our competence or control. Since the Enlightenment we have come from the world of shadows and impotence to the bright sunlight of reason and power. Given enough time, resources and will any problem becomes solvable. We have used this incredible power to enhance the quality of life, and modern medicine has bestowed on us a wealth of miracles. The ultimate enemies to be defeated are suffering and death. In time, the modern medical *credo* holds, this too shall come about. But for now we must do *all* we can to stop suffering. At times this will mean that the direct taking of another's life is considered morally acceptable.

Again the Christian story must counsel another vision for seeing ourselves rightly as creatures of a loving Creator and Redeemer. The human condition is limited, finite and sinful.

We cannot do everything or correct every failing or right every wrong. And we certainly cannot heal every hurt. There comes a point when we must lift up the mystery of suffering and death to our heavenly Father in imitation of Jesus on the Cross. On the surface, it seems noble to claim responsibility for healing all hurts and righting all wrongs. However, such an attitude can be a sign of *hubris* or pride. This moral arrogance leads to the situation (in the words of William F. May) in which we "confer death in order to spare suffering." I am not arguing for quietism or fatalism. While we cannot do everything, we can do something. In the face of suffering and dying we are called to keep fellowship with those who journey a road we all travel.

Finally, consequentialism is attractive because of its simplicity. Those whose loved ones are suffering and dying, need support and courage. Consequentialism seems to offer an easy solution to a complex problem. But as Professor Meilaender reminds us: "For, at least for Christian vision, the fundamental imperative is not 'minimize suffering' but 'maximize love and care.' " To accept the insight of Meilaender we need to risk believing that suffering, when united with Christ, can be ennobling and redemptive. We do not seek suffering as a good in itself, but when suffering comes to us we follow the example of Jesus. When suffering comes to others we stand with them with a love that never allows us to directly end that human life.

Magisterial Teaching

The official teaching of the Roman Catholic hierarchy is contained in three statements: a speech given by Pope Pius XII in 1957 the Second Vatican Council's document, *The Church in the Modern World*; and the 1980 document of the Sacred Congregation for the Doctrine of the Faith entitled, *Vatican Declaration on Euthanasia*. This last document will be discussed separately from the other two. This is because a significant departure from past Vatican statements has taken place. Hence, special treatment is called for.

The first two documents mentioned above clearly express the traditional teaching of the Church relating to euthanasia: namely, that the direct, willful taking of another's life is morally wrong. They base their moral judgments on the following principles:

First, there is a real distinction between the direct termination of human life and allowing one to die one's own death with dignity. The traditional understanding rejects the consequentialist approach and places great moral weight on the means as well as the aim and intention of one's actions.

Second, the distinction between *ordinary* and *extraordinary* is employed. There is no moral duty to employ those means which would place heroic demands on the patient or his family. Only ordinary means are morally required for the prolonging of human life.

Finally, there is an appeal to the principle of double-effect whereby nothing is omitted or directly done to the patient which would bring about his intended death. The patient dies as a result of his illness or injury regardless of our heroic efforts, and not because of any action on our part to kill him. We are not the cause of the patient's death. In fact, it is a sign of great wisdom and trust to withdraw useless non-beneficial medical treatment. We are indicating that physical life is a good but not the highest good. Death is an evil but not the worst evil. There comes a time when we must hand back to God the life he first entrusted to us. Ultimate ownership is not ours. Hence, to know when to let go is a prudence that respects life, shows true love for another, and acknowledges the Lordship of Christ over the living and the dead.

In 1980 the Sacred Congregation for the Doctrine of the Faith issued its *Vatican Declaration on Euthanasia* (this remarkable document is contained at the end of this book in Appendix I). It was well written, sensitive to the contempoary theological scene, aware of pastoral needs, avoided much of the dry formalism of past statements, and moved away from some of the traditional language of past statements in favor of a language which more adequately meets the needs of today's complex-moral world. Father Richard A. McCormick, S.J. called the document "excellent." Professor James Gaffney of Loyola University in New Orleans called it "enlightened and enlightening . . . regarding sensitively to issues as they are actually being raised and to concerns as they are actually being felt." High praise indeed.

What concerns us is the actual teaching of the document itself. I recommend Professor Gaffney's fine study entitled, "The Vatican Declaration on Euthanasia & Some Reflections on Christian Ethical Methodology" (*Thought* Vol. 57 No. 227, December, 1982). Much, though not all, of what follows proceeds from Gaffney's analysis. Naturally, for a better approach the reader is encouraged to read the Vatican's document and Gaffney's article.

The Declaration makes clear that contemporary statements by the papacy remain in effect. What it hopes to do is to apply these statements to the question of euthanasia in light of today's situation. The pastoral thrust is very clear from the beginning. The Declaration is quite short yet is filled with many rich insights. The following is a brief summary of some of the important aspects of the document.

1. The Declaration desires to join with all people of faith and good will in witnessing to the dignity of human life. However, the believer's appreciation of human dignity is grounded in his understanding of life as a gift from a loving God. Hence, because life is a gift there can be no direct killing of an innocent human being. This does not mean that life is an absolute good which demands saving at all costs or at the expense of all other values.

Human life is not idolized. Yet we cannot directly take our own life (suicide) or the life of another. To do so is to take upon ourselves the right that ultimately rests only with God.

2. The Declaration goes out of its way to stress that euthanasia is not morally acceptable at any point along the human continuum of life. From womb to tomb life must be respected and revered. Related to this is the need to decipher the cry of the sick, suffering and dying who may request "to be put out of their misery." The Declaration indicates that this is really a cry for love, care and fellowship in which the patient is forever a person. Such cries of frustration and despair may in reality be pleas for recognition that the dying person is still in need of compassion. The suffering and the dying need to be encouraged to unite their cross with that of Christ in a truly redemptive, healing way.

3. The Declaration's choice of phrases and language is most refreshing. There is an avoidance of slogans which have currently made the bioethical rounds. Also the Declaration is willing to allow in place of the traditional categories—ordinary/extraordinary—the use of "proportionate and disproportionate" means. The Declaration puts it this way:

> In the past, moralists replied that one is never obliged to use "extraordinary" means. This reply, which as a principle still holds good, is perhaps less clear today, by reason of the imprecision of the term and rapid progress made in the treatment of sickness. Thus some people prefer to speak of "proportionate" and "disproportionate" means.

What does the recognition of this "new" terminology mean? This is an especially important issue because of the uneasiness expressed by some over the approach of proportionalism. The Declaration proposes that difficult bio-medical dilemmas be solved through a prudent balancing of values, means (cost, risk to the patient, complexity and availability of the technology), and reasonably expected results. The ability of the patient to sustain (physically and morally) various technologies is no small concern for such medical-moral decision making. The Declaration, following this general proportional approach, does allow for risky experimental procedures. These can be understood as an act of Christian love and responsibility to the human family as a whole. However, the patient retains the right to discontinue these experimental procedures at any time. All in all, the Vatican is counseling prudence.

4. The Declaration closes with a spiritual reflection on sickness and death. Death comes for all and there are limits to our curing powers. The temptation must be resisted to either use *all* means to keep physical life going, or to withdraw human care and love when the limits of curing are reached. The closing words of the Declaration deserve to be written on the heart:

> As for those who work in the medical profession, they are right to neglect no means of making all their skill available to the sick and the dying; but they should also remember how much more necessary it is to provide them with the comfort of boundless kindness and heartfelt charity. Such service to people is also service to Christ the Lord, who said: "As you did it to one of the least of these my brethren, you did it to me."

Other Voices on Euthanasia

The Declaration on Euthanasia indicated that some modern moralists wish to abandon the traditional categories of ordinary/extraordinary means for prolonging life. The Declaration (while still holding to the acceptability of those traditional categories) itself talks about "due proportion in the use of remedies" (section

IV of the Declaration). Furthermore, the Declaration's general spirit is proportional in tone and counsels such an approach (the balancing of values, means and results) in making these difficult medical-moral decisions. A number of contemporary moral theologians and philosophers have offered alternative categories to the traditional ones. In this section we will present the serious and helpful reflections of three such moralists: Father Richard A. McCormick, S.J., moral philosopher Robert M. Veatch, and the Protestant theologian Paul Ramsey.

1. *Richard A. McCormick, S.J.* Father McCormick is one of the Catholic Church's finest moral theologians and has made significant contributions to our thinking in the field of bio-medical ethics. Throughout his many writings he has made the case that we do, in the final analysis, make "quality of life" decisions. Hence, he wants to drop the distinction between "quality of life" and "sanctity of life" approaches to medical-moral problems. Quality of life assessments ought to be made within an overall reverence for life and respect for the sanctity of human life. However, there are times when keeping one alive (which is in reality a prolonging of the dying) is really an insult to life and shows little respect for the person or God. The failure to let go can be an affront to the basic trust we are called to have in the providence of God.

McCormick goes further and makes the telling point that while *EVERY PERSON* is of *EQUAL VALUE* not *EVERY LIFE* is of *EQUAL VALUE*. It is misleading to say that the life of a person in a persistent vegetative state is of the same quality as the life of a person engaged in the normal activities of everyday life. All discrimination (judgment) as to what best serves the dignity and sacredness of life must be made *as it applies to the individual person*. Human life can become of such a quality that it places an excessive hardship on the individual and the family. In the words of Father McCormick: "Our main task is to discover as a community of reasonable persons where the line is drawn and why." This task is crucial and cannot be avoided.

Father McCormick advocates a methodological approach to medical-moral problems that is termed *proportionalism*. This approach involves three elements. Firstly, the suspension of a value is done in the name of a value of equal importance. Secondly, we live in a fallen and tragic world. There are times when the good we desire is not realized. The very evil we hate we catch ourselves doing (see Romans 7). History is broken and there are situations in which a mixture of good and evil (wheat and tares) results from our actions. Hence, we must settle for doing the least amount of harm. Trade-offs must be made if we have found no less harmful way of protecting the values we cherish. Thirdly, when we lay aside a value we always do so with regret. We must guard against allowing the exception to become the rule. We must not only have insight into the present situation but also foresight in trying to determine the impact of our actions on this value in the future.

Father McCormick is holding up a Christian realism which acknowledges the complexity of the world and the human heart. Proportionality is never to be understood as a moral calculus simply adding up the goods and evils. Rather, we are challenged to achieve a certain order of goods; a hierarchy of values which are upheld and sacrificed in light of the patient and the situation. Above all, we must be prepared for "the long twilight's struggle" in the less than brave new world. There are no easy answers to complex issues. Ambiguity is not removed and conscience cannot take a holiday. We must daily struggle in order to be responsible in our decisions. We must be humble enough to realize their imperfection. And we must be trusting enough to allow another to perfect them.

2. Robert Veatch. Mr. Veatch is a moral philosopher who has written the provocative and thoughtful book, *Death, Dying, and the Biological Revolution.* Veatch holds that the terms ordinary/ extraordinary are vague and inconsistent. He proposes that we put ourselves in the place of the patient and employ the terms *reasonable* and *unreasonable* in regard to the means of prolonging life. Reasonable means are any treatments that are deemed *useful* and do not give rise to any significant patient-centered objections based on physical, mental, familial, social, economic or religious concerns. Unreasonable means would be all treatments which one would deem *useless* for this particular patient and his total situation. Veatch believes (and this belief does cause a great deal of trouble today) that what is reasonable and unreasonable can be reached so as to avoid total subjectivism and other abuses.

Veatch applies these concepts of reasonable/useful and unreasonable/useless to the competent and incompetent patient. He concludes that from the patient-centered perspective it should be sufficient for competent patients to refuse treatment whenever they can offer reasons valid to themselves as reasonable persons (reasons of burden related to the physical or mental). Incompetent patients (child, senile, comatose) must have others make various decisions for them. Treatment can be refused by a person on behalf of another if it would "seem within the realm of reason to reasonable people."

Naturally we feel it necessary to ask Veatch, "Just what is reasonable to reasonable people?" Obviously, we will get conflicting answers to this question from different people. Hence, moralists often appeal to the concept of *substituted judgment* (see the excellent article, "Substituted Judgment and the Terminally-Ill Incompetent," by Edmund N. Santurri and William Werpehowski in *Thought* 57, 1982) based on what is in the "best interest" of the patient. But again we are left wondering, "Just what is in the best interest of the patient?" The outstanding physician and moral philosopher Edmund Pellegrino (former President of the Catholic University of America) has suggested that the following four elements be present when speaking of another's best interests:

First, careful attention must be paid to the costs and benefits of various medical treatments employed by the physician. The best interest of the patient is not achieved if we fall victim to medical pessimism or vitalism. The physician must know more than the latest medical techniques. He must know his patient as a person.

Second, much of medical practice involves the physician and the patient (or family) in a discussion of values. The competence of the physician in the realm of medicine does *not* mean that he is any more competent than the patient or family in making decisions about what kind of life has meaning or is worthwhile.

Third, the best interests of the patient are always maintained to the degree that human freedom and informed decision making are enhanced and respected. Whenever possible the patient must be given the freedom and adequate information to make proper medical decisions. Anything less is not in the patient's best interest.

Fourth, the best interests of the patient must take into account what *that* particular patient holds to be the highest good and gives ultimate meaning to his life. People of good will can differ on what that is, and this is to be expected and respected. Often the deepest religious values of the patient come into play. Father McCormick summarizes it nicely: "Therefore judgments of best interests may differ. Reasonable persons may have differing theologies." (See Father McCormick's excellent treatment of Edmund D. Pellegrino's "No Code Orders: Medical Crisis, Medical Choice and Patient Good," in McCormick's "Dignity, Passages, Madness, Suffering and Dying," chapter 6 of *Health and Medicine in the Catholic Tradition*).

3. *Paul Ramsey*. Professor Ramsey is Harrington Spear Paine Professor of Religion at Princeton University. In the field of general ethics, and bio-medical ethics in particular, his contributions are many and lasting. A Protestant, Ramsey speaks a language, and offers a faith, that is ecumenical in its most

universal sense. His self-imposed last book in medical ethics, *Ethics at the Edges of Life*, is a masterpiece.

Professor Ramsey holds that any talk of "quality of life" and "reasonable treatment" sets us on the road to slippery subjectivism. He writes:

> Robert M. Veatch proposes that we translate ordinary/extraordinary into reasonable/unreasonable—that is, treatments for which there is good reason to accept them and treatments for which there is not. He makes very little objective reference, however, into reasonableness or the reasonable man's standard.   (*Ethics at the Edges of Life*)

Furthermore, Professor Ramsey is also uneasy with the traditional terms ordinary/extraordinary:

> There was a final point listed at the beginning of this chapter, namely, you do not need to puzzle for very long over the categorical distinction between "ordinary" and "extraordinary" means of saving life. By that I mean that those terms as classes or categories of treatment are no longer useful and may in fact be helping to open the door to a policy of choosing death as an end. Yet before we can discard the classificatory or categorical meaning of *ordinary/extraordinary*, we shall need to search for adequate replacements. It is easier to criticize and discard the use of that language in treatment refusals than to propose substitutes.
>
> (*Ethics at the Edges of Life*)

Just what replacements to the traditional categories of ordinary/extraordinary does Ramsey propose? He counsels a "medical indications policy" as a superior way of making medical-moral decisions while avoiding the subjectivism that too easily leads to euthanasia. By a "medical indications policy" Ramsey holds that those means which are *helpful* would be ethically required in the prolonging of life. Those means which are *helpless* would not be ethically required. If we are to avoid the subjective use of reasonable/unreasonable and ordinary/extraordinary, we must focus our "attention to the objective condition of the patient, *not* to abstract classification of treatments or to the wishes of any of the parties concerned—not even to the previously expressed opinion (as reported) of Karen Ann Quinlan." The objective condition of the patient calls for a standard *rule of practice* that must be followed. Granted there will be exceptions and rare cases when the standard practice must be altered or abandoned totally. However, we must remember that the exception does not negate the general practice. Ramsey holds that by appealing to the objective medical condition of the patient and the standard medical rule of practice, we erect two crucial barriers against an easy subjectivism which disvalues the life of the weak and dying.

What is one to make of these ethical reflections by three outstanding theologians and philosophers? Personally I share Professor Ramsey's uneasiness concerning the growing subjectivism which has crept into the doing of ethics in general and bio-ethics in particular. Once again I am very appreciative of Father McCormick's labors in the field of medical ethics. However, I find the "quality of life" approach troubling in its subjective implications. Veatch is to be commended for struggling in a serious way with the moral dilemmas each of us face from the biological revolution. Yet I think that Ramsey's critique of Veatch is telling: "*Reasonableness* plainly means in this instance no more than the patient's autonomous subjectivity—a strange use of the term *reasonable.*"

Having said all this about McCormick and Veatch I am also uneasy about Ramsey's approach as well. It seems to me that his medical indications policy can lead to serious abuse. Secondly, his approach claims to rely on the objective condition of the patient and not the subjective wishes or opinions of the patient or others. Ramsey's medical indicator policy can easily lead to medical vitalism in which the physician employs *all* means available (though they may *not* be desired by the patient or the family). This policy seems to place decision making about treatment totally in the hands of the physician. The patient and the family are removed from the decision making process. Also Professor Ramsey believes that the condition of the patient does *not* require interpretation. This, I believe, grants an objectivity to medical diagnosis which it does not enjoy. Physicians of good will and high ethical principles can disagree about the prognosis and treatment of a patient. The standard rule of practice is not always so "clear and distinct" as Ramsey seems to believe. The values, opinions and ultimate good of the patient and family must be taken into account. Decisions about whether to treat or to continue a treatment involve more than the so-called "objective" medical condition of the patient and the standard rule of practice.

What then is left to us for guidance concerning these difficult medical-moral issues? Once again I find myself *for the most part* in agreement with the *Vatican Declaration on Euthanasia*. The Declaration does a masterful job of balancing the medical indicator so prized by Ramsey along with the recognition that there comes a time when certain medical treatments are neither useful nor reasonable. The sacredness of every human life is absolutely maintained while recognizing the key insight of McCormick that every life is not of equal quality. The Declaration takes into account the values and life situation of patient and family. There is more to proper treatment than the state of the art. One must pay attention to the state of the patient in *all* of his or her complexity.

The Legalities of Euthanasia

More and more the complex medical-moral issues of today (and no doubt of tomorrow) are finding their way into courtrooms, legislatures and federal agencies. Such involvement troubles many. They see the current rush to the courthouse or even the White House as medicine by judicial power or "Big Brother" (especially in terms of federal guidelines for the care of the newly born, handicapped or retarded. This will be discussed in the next section). On the other hand, we can see such involvement by our legal institutions as a praiseworthy attempt to exercise their proper function in setting standards for the withdrawal of treatment. However, we must be ever vigilant that our courts and legislatures form opinions and enact laws which respect the dignity of all persons and safeguard the rights of citizens—especially the sick, suffering and dying. Furthermore, on the day to day basis of medical practice we must continue to allow the competent and compassionate physician to care for the patient. No court, legislature or government agency can substitute for the good physician. Medical practice requires quick and prudent decisions that escape the parameters of our slow-moving legal institutions.

As one might expect, the recent judicial and legislative materials concerning euthanasia are both extensive and complex. It lies beyond the scope of this book to present all relevant materials and analysis. Hence, we will have to offer a broad review of the current legal situation. The reader who wishes further information can consult the following: "Euthanasia, The Right to Life and Termination of Medical Treatment: Legal Issues," by Dennis J. Horan, J.D. in *Moral Responsibility in Prolonging Life*; "Right to Die: Legislation: Current Legal Status," by Dennis J. Horan, J.D. in *The New Technologies of Birth and Death* (both books are publications of the Pope John XXIII Center); and "Dignity, Passages, Madness, Suffering and

Dying," by Richard A. McCormick, S.J. in his book *Health and Medicine in the Catholic Tradition.*

The following legal aspects of euthanasia should be kept in mind:

1. At the present time American law considers euthanasia to be an act of homicide. The classification of such acts remains even when the motivation is mercy—the relieving of intense suffering or a prolonged comatose condition. In the legal terminology there is an absence of ill will but not of malice. Legal malice is present when one knows the action to be committed is prohibited by law.

2. Juries are very reluctant to convict those who kill another if it can be shown that the motivation was "mercy"—the relieving of intense suffering. The legal defense is usually grounded in a plea of temporary insanity. Even when the jury returns a guilty verdict judges are reluctant to impose jail sentences. The belief is that the one who performs the act has suffered enough; his or her capacity was diminished; and jail would serve no purpose.

3. The issues of abortion and euthanasia often come together under the slogan of "freedom of choice." Those who advocate voluntary euthanasia do so under the claims to privacy and the freedom to do as one pleases with one's own life. Furthermore, the law should allow and even assist one in ending his life. Again, we seem to be passing from euthanasia liberty to right. This right would impose a duty on society to provide this "service." In time, might this not finally become an obligation? Would the sick, suffering, elderly, handicapped, etc. come, in time, to feel an obligation to step aside and make room for the more deserving? The rising tide of public opinion favoring some form of euthanasia should alert us to the increased efforts for statutory euthanasia.

4. In 1976 the state of California passed the first legislation concerning the so-called "Right to Die"(the California Natural Death Act). The purpose of this legislation is to allow a person to

leave a legally binding statement which outlines his wishes concerning medical treatment—its limits and its removal. Such legislation aims at protecting the incompetent patient from excessive medical intervention by physician or family. Individual states have enacted various forms of so-called living will or natural death legislation. There is a wide diversity among the states. Following California's lead, seven states passed similar legislation. Since 1977 only Kansas and Washington have done so. Recently, various states have written into law some form of natural death legislation (brain-death and/or some combination of brain and respiratory failure). Naturally, the legal situation remains quite fluid.

* 5. The California Natural Death Act of 1976 gave rise to a document called the "living will." Although it takes many forms, essentially the living will directs that all significant others (physicians, clergy, lawyer, family, spouse, etc.) not make use of extraordinary or heroic means to keep one physically alive when there is no *reasonable* (based on the best medically indicated advice) hope of recovery. The person is directing those who love and care for him to do one last act of love—let him die his own death without being subjected to excessive artificial means which will only prolong his dying. The document is signed in the presence of witnesses and copies are distributed to these significant others.

What motivates the writing and even the need for a living will? I think Pope John Paul II in his encyclical, *Redemptor Hominis*, touched on the reason: "What modern man is afraid of is the very work of his hands and, even more so, of the work of his intellect and tenderness of his will." Modern man is afraid of "precisely that part that contains a special share of his genius and initiative" which "can radically turn against himself . . . producing an understandable state of disquiet, of conscious or unconscious fear and of menace." These remarks by the Pope clearly articulate the present condition of modern medicine and the enormous power of technology. Many today are afraid of the very machines that were constructed to enhance life. Instead, they seem to mock us as machines of fear which hold before us the waking-nightmare of an endless dying and unspeakable suffering. None of us can view modern medical technology in the same light since we have been exposed to the tragedy of Karen Ann Quinlan. We want to avoid such a fate for ourselves and our loved ones. In order to do so many are turning to the "living will."

What does prudence counsel about the use of the living will? The theological and philosophical communities are divided on the wisdom of such a document. Those who advocate the living will stress that the living will protects the patient from "over-treatment" through heroic means of life prolongation. Second, the physician does not feel the burden of using *all* means to prolong life in order to avoid a lawsuit or criminal charges of neglect. Third, the living will frees the family from agonizing over such painful decisions concerning the treatment of a loved one. The question—Do we pull the plug?—does not carry the awesome burden it once did. The patient's wishes are spelled out.

Those who object to the living will hold that it gives the false impression that the patient does not *now* have the right to refuse treatment. The patient enjoys these rights (based on human dignity, autonomy and privacy) and they need not be granted by a legislative body. Second, the living will seems to affirm that the physician, not the patient and family, is the main decision maker. For the physician still determines what is useful and useless. Third, no document can possibly cover every situation that may arise. The document gives one a false sense of security. In addition, many states have conflicting laws about death and the treatment of the dying. There is already too much confusion without adding more. Fourth, if there should ever be a federal law concerning the living will, what happens to those who fail to enact one? Are they doomed to useless, heroic treatment? Finally, the formulation of the living will usually is completed when one is well. There is a serious concern about the possibility for changing one's wishes. This is especially crucial for the incompetent or comatose patient.

Naturally, there are no easy answers to hard questions. Yet it seems to me that we should avoid living will legislation. Pope Pius XII indicated in 1957 that the ultimate decision-makers concerning medical care and treatment (its discontinuance as well) are the patient and the family. The physician does not enjoy rights independent from the patient. Unfortunately, the living will leaves the impression that the patient needs to be protected from the physician *by law*. Furthermore, we are led to believe that the right to refuse heroic treatment is something granted by the state. If this "right" is granted, then it can also be taken away. In either case, the inherent dignity and rights of the patient are threatened. Finally, such legislation creates an atmosphere of distrust between physician and patient. The clear impression is given that the physician and his machines must be kept at bay. Such an atmosphere is anything but conducive for healing and patient well-being.

In the Matter of Baby Doe

What follows is in no way a complete discussion, in ethical and legal terms, of the tragic situation of *Baby Doe* or the treatment of defective newborns in general. Rather, a reflection on what it means to care for the little ones who come to us, especially for those who come in ways that demand special love. I hope to accomplish two things: to share and affirm the distinctive Catholic-Christian vision of what it means to love and care for the least of our brothers and sisters; and secondly, to clearly state the Christian vision transcends the demands of a natural humanism. We are challenged and *empowered* to love as Jesus loved. To the world this is foolishness and weakness. To the Christian it is the very power of God as love.

In the spring of 1982 the attention of America became fixed on Bloomington, Indiana. Why? A couple made the decision to allow their defective newborn child to die even though the defect was treatable. The infant was born with Down's syndrome and a defective digestive system; he died of starvation and dehydration. Jeff Lyon in his thought-provoking book, *Playing God In the Nursery*, writes:

> Though Baby Doe's whole existence was compressed into a matter of days, it left more of a mark on the nation than lives of far greater duration. The impact of his death was felt in the White House and in virtually every hospital nursery in the United States, and it triggered a nationwide debate that shows no sign of fading.

This national debate "that shows no signs of fading" ultimately is about how we as a people value life. It touches the deepest core of our being and highlights our moral identity. Debates in the public square have an unfortunate way of turning into pure academic exchanges or intellectual game playing. To do this is to avoid the impact of Baby Doe. Nat Hentoff, a civil libertarian, wrote an excellent article in the January, 1985 edition of *The Atlantic Monthly* ("The Awful Privacy of Baby Doe"). He interviewed Linda McCabe, a registered nurse in the special-care nursery of Bloomington Hospital. She still grieves for the baby and is very frustrated at her inability to save him. She told Hentoff:

> At least I wasn't part of the killing. The other nurses in special care and I told the hospital administration we would not help starve that child. So the baby was moved to

another part of the hospital, and the parents had to hire a private nurse.

Ms. McCabe went on to recount her shock and anger when the orders came forbidding the child to be fed by mouth:

> Who did they think they were—asking me to do something like that? By the fourth day it got so bad, thinking about that baby just lying there, crying, that some of us nurses started checking in law books to see if we could find some legal arguments to stop the killing of that baby. But as it turned out he only had two more days to live.

The tragedy of Baby Doe is compounded with the realization that he did not have to die. The physician of delivery, Dr. James Schaffer, had recommended corrective surgery in order to repair the deformed esophagus. Also, the parents of Baby Doe did not have to be "burdened" with the child. Many families came forward and offered to adopt him. All of this was rejected. Hentoff simply concludes that the parents "did not want a retarded child."

I am not insensitive to the agony, doubts and dark nights of the soul endured by Baby Doe's parents (and no doubt many other parents). Nor do I stand as their judge. Such judgment must be reserved to a higher court whose Kingdom and Constitution are balanced in the perfect blending of justice and mercy. Parents must make these life and death decisions often under the heavy burdens of disappointment, guilt and the absence of a clear moral light. One of the special burdens and graces of parenting is being afforded the opportunity to extend one's marital vows "for better or worse" to that bundle of eternity we call "a child."

I am not saying that the parents of Baby Doe did not "love" their child. I am not saying that parents who make similar decisions are not loving. What I am saying is that the words "love," "compassion" and "care" have a very different meaning when they are illuminated by the Christian story. As Professor Meilaender reminds us:

> Against this background of belief (human life not an absolute good and death and suffering not ultimate evils) we can better understand what *love* and *care* must be within a world constructed in Christian terms. In *this* world no action which deliberately hastens death can be called "love." Not because the euthanatizer need have any evil motive. Indeed, as the case of the compassionate friend makes clear, the one who hastens death may seem to have a praiseworthy motive. Rather, such action cannot be loving because it cannot be part of the meaning of commitment to the well-being of another human being within the appointed limits of earthly life. The benevolence of the euthanatizer is enough like love to give us pause, to tempt us to call it love. And *perhaps* it may even be the closest those who feel themselves to bear full responsibility for relief of suffering and production of good in our world can come to love. But it is not the creaturely love which Christians praise, a love which can sometimes do no more than suffer as best we can with the sufferer.
>
> ("Euthanasia and Christian Vision")

These words of Professor Meilaender are of utmost importance, for they directly answer the argument advanced by Richard B. Broudt (and no doubt supported by many others): "It seems obvious . . . that once the basic decision is made that an infant is not to receive the treatment necessary to sustain life beyond a few days it is mere stupid cruelty to allow it to waste away gradually in a hospital bed—for the child to suffer, and for everyone involved also to suffer watching the child suffer"

("Defective Newborns and the Morality of Termination," in Marvin Kohl's *Infanticide and the Value of Life*). For the Christian there can be a deeper tragedy and blindness behind the decision not to treat. The decision not to treat must never slide us into a justification for a direct ending of innocent human life. We are not allowed to stop suffering by killing the patient. Bioethicist Andrew C. Varga, S.J. has written:

> Promoters of mercy-killing of defective newborns further argue that non-treatment in reality is a means to terminate life and consequently it does not differ from a positive intervention of killing the infant. It was previously pointed out that the morality of non-treatment when there is no affirmative duty to treat the patient is not wrong ethically. In that case the intention is not directed to the violation of the patient's right. In the case of infanticide, however, the intention is directly to kill the infant which is the usurpation of dominion over another person's life.
>
> ("The Ethics of Infant Euthanasia," *Thought* Vol. 57 no. 227, Dec. 1982)

Father Varga goes on to remind us that if we fail to make the distinction between allowing to die and direct euthanasia, we are in reality giving one human being control over the life of another. Furthermore, we are told that infanticide is reserved for special cases. However, we know how exceptions have a way of becoming the rule. There is reason to suspect and fear that what happened to Baby Doe could easily happen to the elderly, the senile, the comatose and all those whom our society finds burdensome. Decisions about the treatment of the defective newborn have their special agony. The words of Father Varga are very helpful: "In some cases it will be difficult to abstract from personal and subjective considerations what will tip the scale in one or the other direction. In the case of well-founded doubt, however, one has to choose the treatment over the non-treatment of the defective infant."

The guidelines advanced by the *Vatican Declaration on Euthanasia* are applicable to the defective newborn. However, when we find ourselves speaking about "the beginning of life" there are a unique set of considerations and existential burdens. Parents love their children. They want their newborn to be happy and healthy. The news of a handicap is especially traumatic. Hence, special care must be extended to parents, and some additional guidelines might prove helpful in making these anguishing decisions. Father Richard A. McCormick, S.J. has advanced the following suggestions as a way of dealing with these most difficult problems. They are especially needed because of the imprecision of the term *handicap*. McCormick offers the following:

1. The omission of lifesaving treatment is not morally permitted for reasons of institutional and familial inability to cope with the infant. The life of the newborn cannot be tied to the emotional, physical or financial capacities of institutions or the parents. To allow otherwise would severely corrode the dignity and sacredness of human life. When the family cannot provide the society must respond.

2. In the matter of Baby Doe it must be clearly stated that mere retardation is not sufficient in itself to withhold lifesaving treatment. To allow the presence of "mere" retardation to account for the withdrawal of treatment is an unjust discrimination. In the words of McCormick this "would mandate fundamentally unequal treatment of equals."

3. McCormick wants to substitute the categories *burden/ benefit* in place of *ordinary/extraordinary*. Life-sustaining treatment need not be employed (or it can be removed) when the effect yields only an excessive burden on the newborn. An important element in decision making is the prognosis by the physician.

4. Life-sustaining treatments may be discontinued (or never even begun) when it becomes evident that the newborn can only be kept alive for a "relatively brief time." The continued use of artificial feeding also indicates that the time may have come for the withdrawal of such treatments.

No doubt to some the above suggestions will seem too slippery and subjective. The terms *benefit/burden* may seem too cold and calculating. To others these suggestions place too much decision-making in the hands of parents and physicians. These worries are not unreasonable. Father McCormick clearly states: "Concrete rules such as these do not mandate decisions. They neither replace prudence nor eliminate conflicts and doubts. They are simply attempts to provide outlines of the areas in which prudence should operate." Allow me to add one easily overlooked point, namely, there is always a "subjective" element in these agonizing decisions. Our feelings, emotions, values and the like come into play. However, we ought not confuse *subjective* with *whimsical* or *capricious*. Even more so, we should not replace the subjective (in the sense of the responsible-acting person in his wholeness) with an appeal to some formula for treatment.

Dr. Anthony Shaw, a professor of pediatric surgery and chairman of the Ethics Committee of the American Pediatric Surgery Association, has devised a so-called "quality of life" formula: $QL = NE \times (H+S)$. Hold on for this one. QL represents the quality of life the child can expect if (!) allowed to live. NE is the natural endowment of the child (physical and intellectual). H stands for the support the child can receive from the home and family. S represents society's contribution (money, education, treatment) to the defective newborn. Nat Hentoff challenged this formula as a means test for deciding who shall live and die. Dr. Shaw rejected this challenge. The formula was devised as a help to parent *and the baby*! Here we go again—we help the baby by killing him. The reader is encouraged to read Mr. Hentoff's excellent article, "The Awful Privacy of Baby Doe," in the January 1985 issue of *The Atlantic Monthly.*

Before moving on, just one question: To whom would you go, or to whom would you send someone in need of guidance, for decision-making concerning the defective newborn: Father McCormick or Dr. Shaw? The answer to that question is much easier than most we face in the nursery today.

Baby Doe: A Brief Legal Note (of Hope)

The Baby Doe case moved President Reagan to action. He ordered that Section 504 of the Rehabilitation Act of 1973 be extended to include handicapped infants. This section clearly states that no institution can discriminate against a handicapped person simply because they are handicapped and still receive federal funds. The handicapped infant must be treated like all the other children in the nursery in terms of feeding and proper medical treatment. The President's order was directed to the Secretary of the Department of Health and Human Services. In order to insure that the presidential directive was carried out, a national hotline was established so that federal authorities could receive and investigate any charges of a handicapped child being denied food and proper treatment.

Unfortunately the presidential order was *vetoed* in court (yes, courts do legislate!) in a 2 to 1 ruling by the United States Court of Appeal for the Second Circuit on February 23, 1984. The Court ruled that Congress did not intend for Section 504 to be applied to Baby Does. The major concern of the Court was the privacy of the parents and child. The government (Justice Department) could not gain legal access to the medical records of a child (in this case Baby Jane Doe in Long Island) who was believed to have been denied proper care. Judge Ralph Winter said in his magnificent dissenting opinion: ". . . a decision not to correct a life-threatening digestive problem because an infant has Down's syndrome is not a *bonafide* medical judgment." Of course it is not. Such a judgment is based on values: what it means to be a good parent, and once again "the quality of life" that we judge this child to be able to enjoy.

The reaction to the Court's ruling was predictable. A great cheer went up from those who mistook the ruling as a victory over Reagan. Others saw this as a victory against "Big Brother" invading the privacy of physician-patient relationships. Yet might it not be that the victory was not over President Reagan but over all the infants who come into our lives with less than perfect credentials? Might not this victory for privacy not drive us deeper into the darkness and isolation which narrows our vision and hardens our heart toward those to be loved? Could it not be possible that our cherished privacy, at times, comes at too dear a price? The fears of "Big Brother" are not easily overcome by substituting the decrees of the "Imperial Judiciary." The handicapped infant often lies in the ditch waiting for some Good Samaritan to be moved to compassion. In Jesus' parable all the likely candidates of concern passed by. Unfortunately, too many likely candidates of compassion pass by the infant today.

The Court of Appeals left an opening for an unlikely candidate to respond to the needs of the Baby Does—the Congress. The Court ruled that the Congress should expressly state that Section 504 applies to handicapped infants. After much debate and a close vote (231-182) The Child Abuse Prevention and Treatment Act was redefined in such a way as to allow the definition of child abuse and neglect to include "the withholding of medically indicated treatment from disabled infants with life-threatening conditions." Of utmost importance, the bill does *NOT* require heroic or extraordinary means of prolonging life (this is crucial from the perspective of the Catholic moral tradition which does not understand life as an absolute value or good). Furthermore, the law requires each state receiving federal money to set up a system for reporting and investigating child abuse as a result of withholding treatment or nourishment. This law clearly recognizes that the newborn is a person in the full Consitutional sense of the term and is not dependent upon parental consent for those rights.

However, the struggle is not over. The American Medical Association, various civil liberties groups and so-called "parent's rights groups" will try to get this law repealed or even declared unconstitutional. That is their right. It is our responsibility to see that the Baby Does are treated with *all* the dignity and respect they deserve as children of God and citizens in the full sense of the term. Nothing more will be required of us and nothing less can be expected.

Suffer Not The Children

Prophets, poets and saints seldom, if ever, live to see their work accepted or their dreams become reality. Such was the case of Pope Paul VI. He had hit upon something that the news media and talk-shows are only now beginning to appreciate. He had detected that much of Western society is anti-child. The world is simply not friendly toward the newly arrived strangers we call children. Paul VI's encyclical letter, *Humanae Vitae*, raised a prophetic voice on behalf of the holiness of marriage, the grace of children and the dignity of all human life. Notre Dame theologian Father James Tunstead Burtchaell, C.S.C. has written: "[Pope Paul VI] sensed that in our time we have come, quietly and gradually, to have a distaste for children . . . The Pope saw something pathological in our culture." Pope John Paul II continued the prophetic message of Paul VI when he visited America in 1978 and reminded us that the gift of a child is the "expression and the fruit of love." Yet we have come to resent and fear the arrival of a child. Why is this so?

Another outstanding theologian, formerly of Notre Dame University, Stanley Hauerwas suggests that our hostility toward children results from our failure to articulate a *moral vision* as to why we have children. Granted that answers abound—duty, fun, love, pressure and simply boredom. However, none of these "answers" suffice. The moral significance of accepting children is that such an acceptance highlights "our willingness to go on in the face of difficulties, sufferings, and the ambiguity of modern life and is thus our claim that we have something worthwhile to pass on. The refusal to have children can be an act of ultimate despair that masks the deepest kind of self-hatred and disgust" ("The Moral Value of the Family"). Our fear of the future is clearly incarnated in our fear of children.

Our contemporary culture has a way of leading us into autism—a very private world of feelings and fear. The autistic person withdraws into an unholy silence that is filled with darkness and self-mutilation. Autism is not confined to the physical and psychological realms but also invades the heart. Our lack of generosity and love keeps our private world comfortable, well ordered, controlled, and fitting like a nice robe and slippers. We resent anything which violates our space. We set up the "NO TRESPASSING" signs for all to see and feel. Children become the most unwelcome of strangers, guilty violators of our space and time. They warp us (or is it that they really stretch us beyond our previously conceived limits of caring?) and in time replace the "NO TRESPASSING" signs with ones that read "NO VACANCY." Children fill up our hearts and challenge us to let our hearts overflow. The vacancies and empty spaces in our lives can be occupied. Our private world is private no longer. Another has moved in and life is never quite the same. What all of this is saying is simple: parents need children if the richer and more complex elements of marital love are to be experienced.

If children have such power in the lives of their parents, so much more do the special children who call forth a special love. The handicapped and weak child lays a unique claim to our love. The Christian vision allows us to see this, and Christian love moves us to action. In order to understand the special love we are called to have for the handicapped and weak, we must situate ourselves within our God-story.

An essential theme of the Christian story is the belief that the God whom we worship and who loves us is a God of weakness and suffering love. Our God does not try to coerce or control us into fellowship with him. He lures and invites us by coming to us as "the fellow sufferer who understands" (A.N. Whitehead). St. Paul puts it thusly:

> Your attitude must be that of Christ: Though he was in the form of God, did not count equality with God a thing to be grasped, but emptied himself, taking the form of a servant . . . he humbled himself and became obedient unto death, even death on a cross. (Philippians 2:5-8)

Our God rejects the kingdoms of this world which rely on violence and death in order to reach their ends. The Kingdom, incarnated and proclaimed by Jesus of Nazareth, is one that comes in weakness and foolishness. The scandal of God's Kingdom is the scandal of vulnerable love that lays itself open to the cross. The God of Jesus, whom we have the courage to call Father, is found not in the citadels of earthly power and position but among the weak, dying, lonely and wretched of the earth.

This God of weakness and suffering love empowers us to love one another as he loved us in Jesus. Those whose lives are formed by the Christian story are drawn in a special way to the handicapped, retarded and weak child. This love is a mirror of the love God has shown to us in Christ. All of us are handicapped and weak. We are all in need of healing and love. God responded to our needs by sending his Son, and so we are to respond to the needs of one another. From the perspective of the Fourth Gospel, when we love one another in weakness and fidelity we make visible God's enduring love. This is anything but sentimental love which is often long on emotion and short on commitment. Rather, in the words of Stanley Hauerwas:

> To love the weak in Christ is to dare to free the weak from our dependency on their need. This love respects the being of the retarded so much that it is willing to allow them to experience the pain and frustration of using their capabilities to come to terms with the world. I do not need to protect my retarded brother with the smothering care that only reinforces his retardation; I can love him with the love that sustains his efforts. He knows this love will not abandon him when he has gone through the struggle to fashion a will independent of mine.   (*Vision and Virtue*)

I would like to bring this small section to a close with a large story of faith and love. Joan and Steve Allison have four beautiful children. One of these beautiful children is Mary Beth. She is a beautiful Down's syndrome young adult. She has lived longer than expected. Her life has not been merely an abundance of days, but her days have been abundant with the giving and receiving of love. Mary Beth has been a master teacher of what it means to love in imitation of the Master Lover. She has taught her two brothers and her sister what it means to be brother and sister in the family of Jesus. She has taught her parents what it means to be generous lovers and to receive the further gifts of marriage that come to those who are lured out of fear into love, love that opens their homes and lives to strangers (Father Burtchaell).

I once asked Joan if she ever regretted her decision to open her life and heart to Mary Beth. She answered with a smile that comes from a baptism of fire and love: "I get tired. The children and my husband grow weary at times. But I don't think we are here on earth to be comfortable. We are here to love so that one day we can be with God who is Love. I really feel fortunate that God sent me Mary Beth. She is *special!* She was a little bundle of heaven and has continued to be so. For Beth has taught so many what it means to love and not count the cost. We have loved and learned every day what it means to love. She has given us much more than we could ever hope to receive."

Euthanasia and Pastoral Care

All of our theological and ethical principles are like straw if they do not school us in living well and help us to love God and serve our neighbor. Our reflections must be incarnated in our lives. Moral energy is released when we have made the story of Jesus our own. Without the connection of head to heart our theology lacks a spirituality. If this is the case, our theology and ethical reflections are like stillborn twins.

This chapter may seem to center around death. Such is not the case. The real issue is life, and what it means for us to be a people of life in imitation of the One who came to give life in abundance. This life in abundance came at a dear price—death on the Cross. The Christian story and vision challenge us to stand with all who face the moment of their own Golgotha. At the hour of their death, we are called to be in solidarity with those who are about to pass into the Unbounded Love of God. Our presence is a witness (often silent and uncomfortable) that says in the language of the Spirit: "Be not afraid. The darkness will give way to life and light. The love our presence signifies is but a taste of the love you will experience from Love itself." To the sick, dying, weak, handicapped and rejected we stand as a family of those wounded but healed.

Browne Barr in his delightful little book, *High-Flying Geese,*

writes about the need for the Christian and the community to
"keep company with the fallen." In order to explain what he
means, Professor Barr tells the following story:

> A child who was late in returning home from an errand
> explained to her worried parents that she had come across a
> friend who had dropped her beloved china doll and it had
> smashed to bits on the sidewalk. "Oh," her father said,
> "You stopped to help her pick up the pieces." "No," the
> child answered, "I stopped to help her cry."

The words of this little girl, "I stopped to help her cry," draw us
into the Christian response to the weak, handicapped and dying.
We keep company with the fallen. We feel their pain and we
allow them to touch our lives as we touch theirs. This is not
sentiment but the strength that allows us to be moved. We keep
company with the fallen because we desire to be the community
of the faithful.

The greatest fear and pain the dying experience is often the
fear of dying alone. The greatest pain comes from dying in a
place of strangers where our name is not known. In a recent
interview Mother Teresa was asked, "Why do you waste all your
time with those whom you know are going to die?" She responded, "How can you say it is a waste? Here is a brother and
sister in need. Here is Christ. Once before these poorest of the
poor die they will experience love. They will know something of
what God is about. This is death with dignity—to die with love."

Although I am a diocesan priest, I live with a Benedictine
community at St. Joseph Abbey. It is the custom of the abbey to
keep company with a brother who is close to death. A member of
the community serves by waiting with the dying as a reminder
that he is not forgotten or unloved. Such treatment is always
considered to be "ordinary." When the power to cure has run its

course, a higher power must come into prominence—the power of caring love.

Most people will not be called to serve with Mother Teresa or live in a Benedictine Abbey. However, the Christian story is one of keeping company with the fallen. The parents, spouses and family members who watch and wait through the seemingly endless night with a dying loved one know this fellowship of caring. The good physician, who knows there are limits to technology but not to the need for compassion, continues the work of the Divine Physician. The nurses and professional staff who treat the patient as a person, follow the example of Jesus who dared to touch the leper in order to make him clean. All of these, and countless others, reveal the healing love of Jesus Christ even though they may never speak his name.

To keep company with the dying is also their keeping company with us. We do not merely give but receive. Father Karl Rahner, S.J. has written that the Christian life is one of following the crucified through the many crosses that come to us: "the experiences of human frailty, of sickness, of disappointments, of the nonfulfillment of our expectations, and so on" (*Theological Investigations* XVIII). The handicapped, weak and dying offer us a special opportunity to experience the limits of all things save one—God's love. When all earthly powers and achievements no longer sustain; when, money, trophies and reputation are of little comfort; then the power of God's healing comes shining through our human weakness.

In the midst of great suffering, the dying of the light, the sting of death and our own powerlessness, the Christian refuses to rebel against life and its Giver. We keep watch with the sick so as to know their strength. Consider the words of Father René Latourelle, S.J.: "In their weakness the sick are strong. They share in the mystery of God's poverty and weakness, for God is never more powerful than in his helpless love: as an infant in

Bethlehem, as crucified on Golgotha, as victim in the Eucharist. Like Christ sufferers have a mysterious power to sanctify those who draw near them" (*Man and His Problems in the Light of Jesus Christ*).

Let us draw close to the handicapped and dying, these special sacraments of God, so that we may know their strength and be sanctified by their witness.

IV
Suicide: The Rejection Of Life

An Enduring Problem

The question of suicide has many forms. It confronts young and old, rich and poor, black and white. Suicide is the second leading cause of death among teenagers. In America as many as seventy persons each day end their lives by suicide. It is the tenth leading cause of death among the general population. The best estimates range from 23,000 to 31,000 successful suicides a year in America. Many feel these figures are very conservative. Any way you add it up, the conclusion is the same: the suicide rate has increased in our society in recent years.

The existentialist philosopher Albert Camus would claim that physical suicide is the cowardly way out. The suicide victim is refusing to face the absurdity of life by ending it all. The only exit that Camus offers is rebellion in the face of absurd existence. However, this is really no exit at all. The very suicide that Camus counsels against seems to be a way out. After all, why endure "the cruel mathematics that command our condition" for no other reason than being authentic? When the rock of our daily existence becomes too much of a burden, the temptation is great to refuse to push anymore. If death is all there is, then it seems we are left with a "resolution of despair." (For more on Albert Camus and his philosophy, see Francis J. Lescoe's *Existentialism: With Or Without God*.)

The Christian story counsels another way. And it is this "other way" we will examine in this chapter. The following aspects of suicide will lay claim to our attention: an overview of the biblical narrative concerning human life; the Christian understanding of freedom; some foundational aspects of suicide; the legal dimensions of suicide; a presentation of official Church teaching concerning suicide along with some contemporary voices on the subject; and finally, some psychological, pastoral and spiritual dimensions of ministering to those who have attempted suicide as well as to the families and survivors of suicide victims.

The Biblical Story: Life and Death and Beyond

The biblical story about man always presupposes an understanding of God. At the heart of the Bible's narrative about God is this: God is life and out of love God shares the divine life with man. In fact, the very life-breath of God animates man and bestows on him his alien dignity. The book of Genesis and the prologue of John's Gospel (the Christian's story of Genesis) come together in proclaiming God as the source of all life:

> The Lord God formed man out of the clay of the ground and blew into his nostrils the breath of life, and so man became a living being.   (Gn 2:7)

> Through him all things came into being, and apart from him nothing came to be. Whatever came to be in him, found life, life for the light of men. The light shines on in darkness, a darkness that did not overcome it.   (Jn 1:3-5)

However, man desires to live apart from God's life-breath and light. Man wills to do his own thing apart from the limits set by God for human freedom. Yet God refuses to give up on the work of his hands. He not only creates but also redeems; through the Spirit, he recreates the face of the earth and turns hearts of stone to flesh. The history of humankind can be understood in terms of God seeking to share his very life with man, and man's desire to live as his own master.

The biblical understanding of man (an anthropology, if you will) contains the following essential perspective: the human person is a unity of mind, body and spirit. While these are three life elements that form the human person—*dam* (blood), *nepes* (spirit), and *ruah* (God's power or life-breath)—the human person is still a whole or unity. It is only in those books of Scripture influenced by Greek philosophy (such as the Wisdom of Solomon), that we are introduced to a dualism or separation of body and soul. For example: "For a perishable body weighs down the soul, and this earthly tent burdens the thoughtful mind" (Ws 9:15).

The Bible places a great deal of significance on blood as life; its loss is death. To shed blood—one's own, another's, an animal's—is to put oneself in the position of God. For only God, who is the author of all life, has the authority to take blood. Biblical scholar Patrick J. Sena, C.PP.S. writes:

> Life is in the blood and thus must be reserved for God—to eat blood is to take upon oneself the position of God as the communicator and giver of life. If the life of an animal belongs to God . . . then the reasoning follows that no human being has a right over the life of any other. Human life is so precious a possession that even an animal bloodletter must be punished. Exodus 21:18 prescribes death for an ox which fatally gores either a man or a woman; even its flesh cannot be eaten for the animal has shed human blood and is thus contaminated.
>
> ("Biblical Teaching On Life and Death," in
> *Moral Responsibility in Prolonging Life Decisions*)

Before moving to the New Testament and the story of Jesus, we need to say something about life after death from the perspective of the Old Testament. The initial Old Testament belief was that after death the person went to a place called *Sheol*. The exact meaning of this term has been much debated by scholars. However, it is usually associated with a place of darkness or the Abode of the Dead under the world. Yet all activity did *not* cease in Sheol. The individual continued a type of "shadow existence." Furthermore, it was believed that all people, regardless of their moral life, went to the same place—Sheol. It is only in the later writings (the deuterocanonical books) that there appears a profound belief in life after death and belief in a separate fate for the just and unjust. For example: "One cannot but choose to die at the hands of men and to cherish the hope that God gives of being raised again by him. But for you, there will be no resurrection to life" (2 M 7:14). The reasons for this shift in thought about the afterlife are many and complex (the question of justice; the influence of Greek culture and philosophy; the belief that God had more in mind than just this earthly life). The reader is encouraged to explore the excellent little book of John Macquarrie, *Christian Hope*.

With the coming of the "Word made flesh" death and afterlife take on a revolutionary new meaning. It is best presented by St. Paul:

> Now I am going to tell you a mystery. Not all of us shall fall asleep, but all of us are to be changed—in an instant, in the twinkling of an eye, at the sound of the last trumpet. The trumpet will sound and the dead will be raised incorruptible, and we shall be changed. This corruptible body must be clothed with incorruptibility, this mortal body with immortality. When the corruptible frame takes on incorruptibility and the mortal immortality, then will the saying of Scripture be fulfilled: "Death is swallowed up in victory."

"O death, where is your victory? O death, where is your sting?" The sting of death is sin, and sin gets its power from the law. But thanks be to God who has given us the victory through our Lord Jesus Christ.   (1 Cor 15:51-57)

The anxiety of death is overcome in the victory of Jesus through the Cross and resurrection. For Jesus' victory over sin and death is a shared victory which he freely and lovingly offers to all who follow him in spirit and truth. Through being one with Jesus in his death and resurrection (Baptism) we become a new being, a new creation. The power of the Old Adam has been rendered impotent. The New Adam, Jesus Christ, has invited humankind to once again tell its story in light of God's story of life.

Physical death does not have the final word in our heart or history. Jesus came to offer us life in abundance. The Incarnation and the Paschal Mystery are the two great narratives that remind us of God's eternal commitment to each of us. In the Incarnation God says "yes" to our human condition by becoming one like us. The shock of the Incarnation is the testimony that God loves us so much that he becomes fully human so that we might become fully alive. The Paschal Mystery continues the revelation of Sinai. "I am who I am" takes on a human face in Jesus. On Sinai the Israelites experienced God's care and involvement on their behalf. On Golgotha the world comes to experience the depth of God's unbounded love for all peoples. God wills that all of his children come to share light and life in abundance in the Kingdom. What awaits those who wait upon the Lord is resurrection and newness of life. Resurrection is not the continuation of earthly existence. Rather, it is a qualitative way of existing in which our earthly life is transformed by the Spirit so that we live the very life of Christ.

The Bible, as we have indicated, reveals that God is the Lord of life and that he wants to share his life with us. God's love and life come to us through the faith community. The whole of the

Bible proclaims that if we are to grow into the likeness of God we do so by sharing a common faith, hope and love in the God who creates, redeems and transforms. In the words of Genesis: "It is not good for man to be alone." The Christian does not view "the other" as a threat, a competitor or a destroyer of our freedom. For the existentialist John Paul Sartre, "hell is others." The Christian is fully aware of egoism and sin, but he also knows that "heaven is others" as well. The gift of faith and the Christian community come to us as gifts that enhance God's basic gift of life. Above all, the Christian community keeps fellowship with the sick, suffering and dying. This is the incarnational way of community, saying that God's love abides and we live to share it.

In light of the Bible, the following can be said about suicide: Because God is the author of all life, the taking of a human life is a very serious matter. The direct killing of the innocent is always a direct challenge to the authority and Lordship of God. The taking of one's own life (suicide) or that of another innocent person (homicide) is a serious violation of God's story for creation. We are called to be a people of life in the service of life. Furthermore, it is never enough for us to merely speak about love and life. We must be living witnesses of God's love. The Church has a responsibility and privilege to continue God's saving love in the world. We must be a people who respect all persons but especially the sick and dying. Without love and respect for human life, we cannot grow into the full measure of our humanity. Pope John Paul II has written:

> Man cannot live without love. He remains a being that is incomprehensible for himself, his life is senseless, if love is not revealed to him, if he does not encounter love, if he does not experience love and make it his own, if he does not participate intimately in it. This, as has already been said is why Christ the Redeemer "fully reveals man to himself." This is the human dimension of the mystery of the Re-

demption. In this dimension man finds again the greatness, dignity and value that belong to his humanity.

(*Redemptor Hominis*)

The direct taking of one's own life or of other innocent persons is not the Christian way of understanding love and care.

Christian Freedom

The modern notion of freedom from obligation and commitment, along with the drive to maximize sheer choice, has serious consequences for the ways we relate to one another and ourselves. We come to understand ourselves, in the words of Eric Fromm, as a "marketing personality." Life is for the consumer to pick and choose as he pleases—from one's car to one's friends and spouse. There is no hierarchy of values and choices. What is crucial is *that* one chooses and not *what* one chooses. The ends are not important. The important aspect of freedom is interior: that is, choices must have an intense desire associated with them. Such a notion of freedom is silent about the end towards which one's intense desire aims. Others become obstacles which negatively affect my freedom and limit my choices. Hence, I must choose my "friends" only in terms of self-interest and choice. Those that enhance my "freedom," so understood, are kept (owned/possessed) and those that burden me are discarded.

The Christian understands freedom in a fundamentally different way. He holds that the contemporary notion of freedom is essentially flawed. Jesuit theologian René Latourelle writes:

The error of atheistic humanism is not its claim that the supreme development of man takes the form of peaceful freedom; that, after all, is precisely the summit to which God is leading us. Its error is its claim to attain by its natural resources alone the deification or perfect freedom to which it aspires. Christianity, on the contrary, tells us that God alone possesses perfect freedom by his very nature, but also through Jesus Christ man is given this perfect freedom if he consents to receive it. As a model for all, Christ enters this realm of freedom which all in our day are feverishly seeking. Christianity sets before us a perfect freedom which completes all and each and brings them to their fulfillment . . . God's initiative in Jesus Christ is in the form of an invitation to enter into that space in which our freedom can uphold to the point where it is deified.

(*Man and His Problems in the Light of Jesus Christ*)

Authentic freedom is never unqualified or "free floating." Christian freedom, true human liberation, comes, not by creating our own world of values and norms (Nietzsche), but through loving obedience to God's freedom revealed in Christ. God has a dream for our world, history and individual lives. Maturity is not understood as the ability to simply choose and overcome others. Maximum freedom comes to those who are able to make an ultimate commitment to God's story for our lives. Only the free man and woman can say: "Let it be done to me as you say" and "not my will be done but thine be done." This is the risk-taking of the truly free who come to know that freedom is never choices about consumer products but the liberty to take responsibility for the kind of person we become by our decisions.

The reason we are so fearful of genuine freedom is that it calls for us to live in a manner which Stanley Hauerwas terms "out of control":

For "living out of control" is but a way of suggesting that we are an eschatological people who base our lives on the knowledge that God has redeemed his creation through the work of Jesus of Nazareth. We thus live out of control in the sense that we must assume God will use our faithfulness to make his kingdom a reality in the world . . . no one is more controlled than those who assume they are in control or desire to be in control . . . All of us in one way or another willingly submit to the illusion that we can rid our world of chance and surprise. Yet when we do that our world becomes diminished as we try to live securely rather than well.   (*The Peaceable Kingdom*)

Hauerwas has put his finger on our modern illusion and discontent when it comes to freedom. Proud modern man lives under the illusion that he is all-powerful and totally free to do as he pleases. Control is defined in terms of money, power, a rising GNP, more missiles or sex appeal. On the other hand, the Christian story holds that true freedom comes to those who submit to and obey God's story.

The modern notion of freedom has significant consequences for the understanding of the *meaning* of our life. Is our life a gift or a possession? The modern answer is clear: I own my own body. I am free to do what I will with my body and life as a whole. There is a loss of the sacred or transcendental point of reference to individual existence. Such views of freedom and life are present in the abortion debate. The woman is free to do as she pleases with her body. She should have unrestrained control over her reproductive powers. The rights of the unborn and of parents and fathers have little, if any, impact.

The modern understanding of freedom and of one's life as a possession also impacts on the issue of suicide. Contrary to what St. Paul writes to the Romans, modern man believes he has an absolute right to control his fate. Each person comes of age by being his own master. When life becomes too burdensome or painful, or when it loses its meaning, we have a right (some would say a duty) to end it. The ultimate meaning, value and purpose of one's life is determined solely by the individual. However, such an autonomy fails to consider the real nature of man's situation—namely, that to be human is to be finite, limited, conditioned and fallible. Our life is a gift that we are called to reverence and love. In so doing, we show reverence and love for the One in whose image we are wonderfully made.

Before us are two ways of understanding and experiencing freedom: the way of modernity or the way of the Christian story. Again the words of Father Latourelle:

> Individuals use their freedom to immure themselves in their world (money, power, pleasure), and then they abide in darkness and become slaves of the idols they have made; or else they acknowledge their poverty, like the "little ones" for whom the kingdom is meant, and open themselves to God in whom they recognize the Absolute One, and then they are free in relation to the world and its idols. The only true freedom is that of the *children of the Father*, those who like Christ have within them the spirit of sonship who makes them say: "Father . . . what thou wilt" (Mk 14:36).
> (*Man and His Problems in the Light of Jesus Christ*)

Fundamental Concepts

The word "suicide" comes from the Latin *suicidium* which means the taking of one's own life. Also suicide is direct and intended and voluntary. The person who commits suicide does so for a number of reasons, ranging from pain to depression to a total loss of meaning. The reasons for suicide are complex and there are certainly no simple answers. One thing is certain—the figures are alarming. The suicide rate doubled between 1960 and 1970, and is now the second leading cause of death among teenagers (see the article "Suicide," in *The Encyclopedia of Bio-ethics*).

Moral theologians usually make several distinctions when speaking of suicide. There are four general categories most commonly encountered: positive, passive, direct and indirect suicide. Positive suicide is the performance of an act in order to bring about one's own death. Passive suicide is the refusal to take steps considered to be ordinary and normal for one's health and recovery.

Direct suicide is a violation of God's command not to kill and is never allowed morally. Traditional Catholic morality has held that direct suicide is intrinsically evil—that it is an evil *act* in itself regardless of the external circumstances. Naturally, we are not passing judgment on the guilt of the one who commits the act. Rather, we are saying that the physical act itself, its very structure and goal, goes directly against God's will of life.

Indirect suicide is defined as the laying down of one's life in which death is not directly intended but certainly foreseen as possible or even probable. Indirect suicide is generally forbidden since traditional moral thinking makes it a wrong even to place one's person in unreasonable risk. However, there are *some* instances when indirect suicide is *tolerated* (yet this toleration is not an endorsement of the situation but a compromise given the fallen, tragic nature of man and history). The *New Catholic Encyclopedia* lists the following standard situations in which indirect suicide may be permitted: the good of the community may call for a leader or specially trained person (such as a physician during an epidemic) to risk his life; the spiritual welfare of another may call for heroic action such as in time of war when chaplains bring the Sacraments; the need to remain true to virtue and faith may call for a martyr's death; and finally, one could risk one's life helping others achieve the worldly goals of freedom, self-respect and truth. Volunteering for experimental and risky medical operations can be justified in the name of helping those who come after (witness the heart transplant patients).

Durkheim, a sociologist, outlined three major categories of suicide. The first type is called *egoistic suicide*. The person who commits or is prone to egoistic suicide is one who lacks a healthy set of interpersonal relationships. The "loner" is a classic example. Durkheim's research indicated that single persons are more prone to suicide than married couples. The second type is termed *anomic suicide*. This person experiences no sense of belonging to society—its community, values, goals and dreams. This person is marginal and lives on the fringes of the community. There is an absence of social bonding. And finally, Durkheim wrote about *altruistic suicide*. This is the opposite of the anomic life. The individual over-identifies with the community and willingly commits suicide for its goals and honors. Naturally in all of these categories there is a complex interaction of many factors such as values, personal beliefs, group integration, social mobility, and the social degree of tolerance for expressions of anger and frustration.

The father of modern psychiatry, Sigmund Freud did not look outside of man but within his very heart (psyche). Freud understood suicide to be a serious breakdown of the ego-defenses which release powerful forces of death (*thanatos*) and destruction. The bubbling cauldron of emotions comes over the top and violently expresses itself in the form of self-destruction (the so-called "death wish"). Freud went on to list many reasons for this hostility to break through: self-hatred, impotence, loss of a loved one, rage at one's inability to control one's environment in order to achieve desired outcomes, and the experience of a terrible injury to one's self-image (Narcissistic trauma).

More and more, we see the courts and legislatures taking an active role on the question of suicide. Much of our traditional legal and social morality is being challenged in new and not always reassuring ways. Let us turn our attention to some of the legal dimensions of suicides.

Suicide: A Brief Legal Jog

Legal involvement (courts and the legislatures along with Congress and the White House) with suicide is enormously complex and varied. It is beyond the scope of this book to explore all the relevant decisions and statutes relating to suicide and the so-called "right to die" movement. Therefore, we must limit our discussion to some of the more prominent cases and laws. The motivated reader is encouraged to follow up this area of concern through the extended bibliography found at the end of this book.

What is America's national past-time? Baseball? No. It is the manufacturing of *rights* (see the excellent article, "The Rights Game" by Walter Goodman in the March 1985 issue of *Harper's*). Rights have become so numerous and individualized that, in the view of Professor Richard E. Morgan, America is being disabled. Morgan holds that one of the most powerful industries in our society is the "rights industry" (the Supreme Court and various interests groups) which has brought us near the point of paralysis as we more and more seek relief in the courts. The notion of the common good and the subordination of private concern for community welfare is lost. In recent times we have witnessed increased efforts to have recognized in law "the right to suicide." Such a "right" would be very troubling. For as sure as the night follows the day, the right to suicide would easily pass into voluntary euthanasia and finally to the "duty to suicide or euthanasia" (a prominent political figure recently spoke about the duty of the elderly to die in order to make room for the new generation). See the excellent book, *Life and Death with Liberty and Justice,* by Germain Grisez and Joseph M. Boyle, Jr. At present the law forbids acts of suicide and euthanasia but as we indicated earlier (in Chapter III), the attitude of the American people has become increasingly permissive.

The "rights game" is played by various interest groups and lobbying concerns. A prominent group which advocates suicide and euthanasia is the Society for the Right to Die. This society has long been involved in trying to pass so-called "death with dignity" legislation. Such legislation would legally permit the taking of one's own life or that of another. Furthermore, the society, through the judiciary and legislative branches of government along with an education program to influence public opinion, seeks to enact *assisted* forms of euthanasia and suicide. There is even the possibility that euthanasia could be performed *without* the consent of the person. Legal safeguards are sought to protect those who assist a person carrying out their "right" to suicide or euthanasia.

Two acts by state legislatures, California and Arkansas, have received a great deal of attention in bio-medical literature. What follows is a brief review of each of these statutes. The state of California was the first to pass a "right to die" statute. This Act stipulates that the adult must be in a "terminal condition" before the physician can carry out his wishes to be left to die with dignity. The phrase "terminal condition" is understood as an incurable condition brought on by illness, disease or injury for which there is no reasonable hope of cure and for which the application of life-sustaining procedures only prolongs the dying. A life-sustaining procedure is one that takes the place of a vital bodily function through the use of a machine or some artificial means. Such procedures are useless as determined by the physician according to the standards of acceptable medical practice, and only prolong dying while robbing the patient of his dignity as a person.

What is one to make of this Act? In and of itself it does not morally violate our respect for life, nor does it undermine crucial values of our western legal and philosophical systems. Yet there must be a constant vigil that such laws based on "right to die" rhetoric do *not* become the wedge that moves us into euthanasia (involuntary or not) and suicide. Legal scholar Dennis J. Horan, J.D. puts it thusly:

> When truly limited to a "terminal condition" under the standards stated in the California Act, such legislation, although unnecessary, does not violate any of the legal values we seek to preserve. It does not legalize mercy killing or assisted suicide. It does not leave the aged defenseless, or the handicapped newborn at risk. It does not destroy the ethical basis of medicine: "to do no harm" Under these circumstances, our concern must be to see that these safe-guards are not changed by amendment. However, other acts which have not been so carefully drafted do not contain even these most basic of safeguards.
>
> ("Euthanasia, The Right to Life and Termination of Medical Treatment: Legal Issues," in *Prolonging Life*)

One such act which causes much concern was drafted by the Arkansas legislature. The morally troubling aspect of the Arkansas act is contained in section two which allows for the withdrawal and non-employment of artificial, extraordinary, radical or extreme means of prolonging life. The difficulty lies in the fact that the law does *not* state that the illness must be terminal. Also, there is a great deal of fuzziness when it comes to defining the key terms of "extraordinary," "radical," and the like. One could picture this statute being interpreted as the state's recognition of the right to commit suicide or euthanasia. Granted that this is *not* what the legislature intended, a tighter wording and explanation is necessary in this case. No doubt the Arkansas courts will be busy helping to determine just what the legislature had in mind.

Another troubling aspect of the Arkansas statute is contained in section three which allows for a parent or guardian to carry out the wishes of anyone (minors, too) who is mentally incapable "or who is *otherwise* incapacitated" (just what this means is open to wide interpretation and abuse). The Act even goes so far as to allow a majority of children to carry out the wishes of a parent if the spouse will not or is unable to do so. Again in the opinion of Horan: "It [the Arkansas statute] is tantamount to the legalization of euthanasia which, under American law, is homicide. It is this type of statute that illustrates the dangers in death legislation, which must be carefully monitored at every legislative level."

The courts have come to play a significant role in the "right to die" and the "right to refuse medical treatment." The courts have made an increasing use of the right to privacy for the refusal of medical treatment (the abortion decision of *Roe v. Wade* made abundant use of this "right" as well). Privacy served as the basis for the Quinlan case. This appeal to privacy as a constitutional right or as granted by the legislature is unnecessary. The right to refuse medical treatment is granted to the person on the basis of common law (torts). Except for emergency situations, the competent adult has the right to refuse treatment even if the refusal brings on death. Naturally there are some overriding considerations such as the need of the state to prevent suicide; the state's role as the protector of human life; and the need of the state to uphold the ethical foundations of medical practice which promote the life and well-being of the patient. The refusal of medical treatment by a competent adult has *not* been legally considered suicide, hence the physician is guilty of neither abandonment nor of abetting suicide.

However, many legal scholars are troubled by the recognition of the right to refuse treatment in the right to privacy. For it has been noted that the Supreme Court has never asserted that a right to refuse treatment exists in the Constitution. The assertion of this new right—the right to refuse medical treatment as a constitutional right—has escaped the Brethren so far. Yet as the rights industry continues to churn away, we can only wonder.

The courts have shown a strange desire to become involved in medical-legal questions. In a famous case, *Saikewicz*, the court held that *court approval* must be obtained before any decision concerning the withholding of treatment be carried out! In effect, the court becomes the final arena of decision making, and the final one who makes the decision, as to what medically should be done for the patient. This is raw judicial power in the extreme; practicing medicine without a license; and is downright unworkable in the everyday realities of hospital and emergency room medicine. Hence, a Massachusetts appellate court moderated the *Saikewicz* ruling (*Dinnerstein*) by holding that judicial review need be sought only when there are life-saving/prolonging measures available and the decision is made *not* to use them. In this way the court hopes to protect the rights of the patient.

The courts have ruled in a number of other significant cases: *Earle Spring, Brother Fox, Starar,* and *Severns*. It is beyond the scope of this book to examine each case. However, a number of moralists and legal scholars have addressed these cases in depth. I would recommend two very fine summary articles published by the Pope John XXIII Center, both written by Dennis J. Horan, J.D.: "Right to Die" and "Euthanasia, The Right to Life and Termination of Medical Treatment: Legal Issues" in *Moral Responsibility in Prolonging Life Decisions*.

In the midst of these many cases, a legal and judicial consensus seems to be emerging. The following aspects of this consensus are significant:

1. The physician has the authority to terminate medical treatment on behalf of the incompetent patient, after deciding that such treatment is useless according to standard medical practice. To terminate such treatment in no way makes the

physician an accessory to the death of his patient. Rather, he is simply allowing the natural processes to proceed uninhibited by useless treatment.

2. In legal terms "useless treatment" is one that does not enhance a reasonable hope for recovery. The patient and physician are not required to employ useless treatment. A very important area of concern is the withholding of food and drink from the patient who is terminal and close to death. The withdrawal of food is seldom, if ever, to be allowed. Liquids serve as a means of comfort to the dying patient.

3. The right and duty of the physician to withdraw useless treatment without fear of civil and criminal penalties must be protected. This protection should not reside in the right to privacy. Rather, the physician simply does not have a responsibility to invoke useless treatment. The physician is *not* the cause of the death. There is no need to invent a right to refuse medical treatment when there is an already accepted practice of not using useless means.

4. The intersection of medicine and law is a complex one. There needs to be dialogue between the two communities but also mutual respect and trust. The physician must be trusted to use his medical judgment for that which promotes the well-being of the patient. The courts should be involved only as a last resort when the physician is acting outside the standards of normal medical practice or if he violates the "canons of loyalty" he owes to the patient. However, the physician should not be forced into practicing defensive medicine because he fears litigation or charges of malpractice.

The recognition by the courts and some state legislatures of the right to refuse useless medical treatment is not unappreciated by the Catholic moral tradition. It cannot be stated enough (since most people simply do not state it properly) that the Catholic moral tradition has long recognized the right of the patient to refuse useless or extraordinary means of prolonging life. When the competent patient freely decides that his time has come and medicine can do no more for his recovery he has every right to let the disease or illness take its natural course. Life is not an absolute value. The competent patient who refuses such useless treatment is not guilty of suicide.

Likewise, the incompetent, comatose or minor patient need not be exposed to useless treatment that clearly offers no reasonable hope of recovery and merely prolongs the dying. To make the decision to withdraw such treatment is not an act of euthanasia. The decision is *not* being made to directly kill the patient; the patient is simply being freed from those machines and procedures which do not promote his or her well-being. This is not an act of homicide.

What we should hope and work for is a consensus among physicians, the legal community and society as a whole that we all must respect the dignity of all persons and their right to life. When the time comes for death, may it find us watching with the dying in a caring and respectful way. Life is not the greatest good, and death is not the greatest evil. While we should not hold on to earthly existence at all costs, neither should we fail to promote life. May we always respect ordinary means of promoting the patient's welfare.

Church Teaching

The Catholic moral tradition has been consistent and clear on the subject of suicide: it is the wrongful taking of one's own life, a serious challenge to the sovereignty of God as the author and giver of all life. In 1980 the Sacred Congregation for the Faith issued its excellent statement on euthanasia (*Declaration on Euthanasia*) which included the following:

> Intentionally causing one's own death, or suicide, is therefore equally as wrong as murder; such an action on the part

of a person is to be considered as a rejection of God's sovereignty and loving plan. Furthermore, suicide is also often a refusal of love for self, the denial of the natural instinct to live, a flight from the duties of justice and charity owed to one's neighbors, to various communities or to the whole of society—although, as is generally recognized, at times there are psychological factors present that can diminish responsibility or even completely remove it.

However, one must clearly distinguish suicide from the sacrifice of one's life whereby for a higher cause, such as God's glory, the salvation of souls or the service of one's brethren, a person offers his or her own life or puts it in danger (cf. John 14:14).   (*Declaration on Euthanasia*)

This is morally consistent, solid and pastorally sensitive. The Declaration upholds the sacredness of human life and the sovereignty of God as the giver of life. Furthermore, there is an excellent sensitivity to some of the reasons for suicide. Note especially the statement that the person who attempts or commits suicide is one who lacks self-love. Self-hatred is very prevalent in our society today. The feelings of being unworthy, lacking in acceptance and inferiority plague many. The churches have a special ministry and opportunity in helping to restore the feelings of self-worth and self-respect. We must make a special effort to extend the kiss of peace, the oil of gladness and the embrace of reconciliation to those who live on the fringes of society and churches. We must find creative ways to make room for so many who have written off life and God's love. Authentic teaching requires *action*. We must make incarnate God's *continuing* love for all people. The faith we proclaim holds that God is love, and that the proof of this love is the gift of life. This proclamation will only be heard over the noise of society and the inner voice of self-hatred to the degree that we love the brokenhearted.

Suicide is often considered to be the ultimate act of individualism. The individual decides, in grand isolation, to take his or her own life. However, the Declaration reminds us that human acts have social consequences. This is of crucial importance for a society which so values privacy, individuality, personal rights and individualized views of liberty. Suicide weakens the bonds of society and its duty to uphold respect for all human life. A society's strength is not measured merely in terms of the GNP and the balance of trade. Moral strength is evidenced by society's respect for human life and the degree to which it protects the life of its most vulnerable members. Society should actively seek to strengthen the bonds of life and relationship between individual members and groups in order to promote the common good.

The Declaration, in addition to being morally responsible, is also pastorally sensitive. There are persons who suffer psychological trauma which diminishes their capacity for sound judgment and weakens the will. These persons do not deserve our condemnation but our loving compassion in imitation of Jesus who was close to the brokenhearted. The Declaration still upholds the objective wrongness of the act, but as to the subjective aspects of guilt and responsibility that judgment is reserved for God. There may even be instances in which the person is so psychologically impaired that there ceases to be any moral culpability at all.

Finally, the section dealing with suicide in the Declaration maintains the distinction between suicide and the greater love that calls for the laying down of one's life. There may come a time in our life when the glory of God, the salvation of souls and the needs of another will challenge us to make this heroic sacrifice. The intention is not to die or to end one's life but to give praise to God as well as service to our neighbor. The Declaration is reminding us once again that our earthly life is *not* an absolute value which must be preserved at all costs. Other values come into play and call for heroism on the part of God's family. It concludes the statement about suicide with a citation from the Gospel of John: "You are my friends if you do what I command you" (Jn 15:14). What Jesus commands of us is love as he expressed it on the Cross.

Theologians and philosophers who approach the question of suicide from a consequentialist perspective will arrive at a different answer. Such a position looks at the results or the end of a given act or process. Since the terminal patient is going to die anyway, what is so morally objectionable about hastening their death and bypassing the suffering and pain of the family? Why must we wait until "nature takes its course"? Would not suicide be a "rational choice"? This temptation to condone suicide must be resisted. The result may be the same—the person dies—but the intention or aim of the act is different. The act of taking one's life as a way of avoiding suffering is disordered. It claims a right over life that the person cannot morally make. For life comes as a gift and is offered as a trust, which makes the act of self-destruction improper. Suicide is an unacceptable way of returning the gift back to the Giver. Suicide is the self-granting to the creature of powers that are reserved for the Creator. There are situations in life which we must tolerate, endure and suffer in hope. We may have the power to bring about our own end, but we do not have the authority.

Other theologians and philosophers have attempted to address the question of suicide from the perspective of proportionalism (while not a strict proportionalist, Catholic theologian Daniel Maguire, in his *Death by Choice*, offers a provocative way of discussing euthanasia and suicide). The proportionalist holds that certain acts are *pre-morally* evil or disordered (ontic evil). The moral significance of the act is known only as we know the circumstances which surround a given act. Suicide is considered to be an ontic or *pre-moral* evil. However, it is only later, after the facts are in, that we can determine the moral quality of the act.

Hence, there may be proportionate reasons or circumstances that would justify suicide.

The approach of the Declaration seems more morally solid. There are human acts which are so disordered that no set of circumstances can alter their deficiency. Suicide is one such act, for it goes against the recognition of God as the Lord of Life and against the gift of life itself as a primary good. The direct taking of one's life cannot be condoned or praised. However, there are circumstances which diminish the moral guilt imputed to the actor. There is an objective order of morality which humans can discover and obey. Likewise, since we are finite, broken and temporal beings we are in need of compassion and love. Those who commit suicide are performing a gravely disordered act but the person may be gravely diminished in the faculties of judgment and will. We find ourselves upholding the importance of human acts while imitating the compassion of Jesus.

The Christian story—our foundational story from which our ethical reflection must flow, be informed and be purified—is one that upholds the dignity of all persons. We are called not only to provide ethical principles but also to be a Church of love and compassion. Professor Daniel Maguire has written:

> The prime moral reaction to suicide should be to attack the causes that yield such bitter fruit. Those of Christian persuasion should be in the forefront here. For Christians, the loss of hope is an apostasy and to contribute to the loss of hope in others is the elementary Christian sin.
> ("The Freedom to Die," *Commonwealth*)

Maguire goes on to discuss "the possibility of objectively moral suicide." While not sharing Professor Maguire's conclusions, I do share his concern for those who feel hopeless. We must make sure that we don't contribute to "such a bitter fruit." I personally do not believe that suicide is a source of comfort for those contemplating it or who feel burdened by life. In the upcoming section we will explore some life-giving and hopeful ways of keeping company with the fallen in our midst.

Miles Yet to Run

Claire was a popular, bright and caring high school senior. Her parents both worked at their professions but provided a home that was rich both materially and spiritually. Claire had two older brothers; both of them attended college on the East Coast. The past tense is being used when writing about Claire, because she has committed suicide. Claire has become a part of a growing national concern—namely, that our young people are killing themselves in alarming numbers. More than a national problem or statistic, Claire was a daughter, a friend, and forever a child of God.

Claire's story is not uncommon among young people her age. She did well in school; had many friends; was preparing for college; and seemed to have everything going for her. And yet . . . her parents found her dead from a gunshot wound, self-inflicted, to the brain. There was no note of explanation or blame. If there had been one, perhaps it would be easier to understand the tragic death of a person who had miles yet to run. To this day Claire's parents wonder why. What did they do wrong? Claire's friends were shocked. Could they have been more sensitive to her needs? Teachers felt they should have seen the "signs," but none seemed present. Enough guilt to go around, but not many answers.

We do know that teenage suicide and attempted suicide is on a dramatic increase. More than 4,000 young people each year take their lives. Another 400,000 try. Suicide is the second leading cause of death among teenagers and young adults ages 15 to 24. We also know that many young persons are involved in slower forms of suicide through drug and alcohol abuse. We know some of the causes—both within the individual (self-hatred, failure, fear of failure, bad relationships, mental disorders, and countless others) and social (achievement orientation, materialism, loss of religious values, breakdown of traditional institutions of support, and the availability of too much too soon). Many of our children are victims of *success*. Great emphasis is placed on winning and being number one. When they achieve a measure of success, there is often pressure to continue to succeed so as not to waste one's talents or let anyone down. The pressure builds with each successive victory to do it again and to do it better than before. A sense of accomplishment is never experienced, as one always must climb to new heights of success. Sometime these heights are too great, and the fall is tragic for all concerned.

Among the most basic of human needs (and this is especially true for the younger person) is that of acceptance which promotes a healthy sense of self-worth. The Christian story is one of *grace* and free acceptance so that we might then learn to walk upright as God's children. God's healing love is never earned or merited. We don't stand before God demanding our just rewards. We have none. Rather, we stand before him in need and dare to call him "Father." Jesus told us to go to the Father in this way because he gives us what we truly need. The gift of Jesus is God's total acceptance of us as we are and as he will re-create us. But first God comes to us and accepts us in our humanity. Before him there is no need for boasting. Before God we come as we are, asking that as poor sinners we may be received into his presence.

The Church which claims the story of Jesus as foundational must structure community life and values in a like manner. We need the acceptance, forgiveness and challenge of one another. We do not need to stand in one another's presence with our trophies, accomplishments, grade point average or press clippings. We stand there as we are—brothers and sisters of a common Father, Redeemer and indwelling Spirit who makes all things new. We don't need to play roles. We can risk intimacy and caring, knowing that there is One who has gone before us to prepare the way into eternal life.

Our young people need a reason to live and a vision that will once again allow young men to dream dreams and young women to prophesy. Young people need a story which will allow them to tell the story of their lives in a more authentic, honest and life-respecting way. The Church offers the story of Jesus and the Kingdom as the way into living life to the full. In the midst of stereo music and endless idle talk comes God's Word of acceptance and hope. We are overfed but undernourished by the bread of this world, but the Lord's table is spread before all who come to worship in spirit and truth. And in a world of brief encounters of the most superficial kind, the Christian community proclaims and lives a love that is faithful, respectful and modeled after the sacrificial love of Christ.

In many ways our young people are like the crippled man who asks Peter and John for some money (Ac 3:1-10). The apostles have a richness far greater and more lasting. It is the name of Jesus Christ. The man will beg and be crippled no longer. The young are asking their elders to give them a vision and a hope. Money, popularity, power, sex, prestige, are not sufficient. They want more. What more *can* they want? They want to know that God is love. The best proof of that is the way we love one another and share the vision of Jesus with others. It sounds so simple. But often, what keeps us from sharing and responding is that we are afraid it is too good to be true. We will have to let go of our demons and idols we have worked so hard to master and build. Yet they do not give life. Only in Jesus Christ do we come to know the joy and peace of total acceptance.

Francine Klagsbrun has written an excellent little book on teenage suicide entitled, *Youth and Suicide: Too Young to Die.* At the end of her book she writes the following:

But changes in society develop over time. And every day ten more young people take their own lives; a thousand more attempt to. If just one extra life can be saved because a friend has learned how to help, if just two suicide attempts can be avoided because parents have picked up clues, a beginning will have been made.

The Christian story is full of episodes in which the lost is found; the dead come back to life; the unaccepted find welcome; the poor are proclaimed rich; the lepers are cleansed; and the ninety-nine are left in search of the one who has gone astray. We see in Ms. Klagsbrun's caring words a page from the Christian narrative—the most precious number is one, and the least of our brothers and sisters is most prized. Let us as a community of faith be about this "beginning" in the name of life.

A Psycho-Pastoral Note

The parish priest, the chaplain in a school or university, and the pastoral counselor in a hospital setting encounter many people with various forms and degrees of depression. The troubled marriage, the pressures that abound in schools, and the suffering that afflicts us all gives rise to feelings of anger, depression, despair and self-destruction. Naturally, we want to help. We are in the "people business" and we want our service to make a real difference. Yet human behavior is highly complex and prudence is essential for proper counseling and direction. This is especially true when we are dealing with the severely depressed person and one who has threatened suicide or seems to be a good candidate for self-destruction. Knowing our limits and not trying to be all things for the person is crucial.

Dr. Michael E. Cavanagh, a clinical psychologist, has written an excellent article entitled, "Cautions in Pastoral Counseling"

(*Human Development*, Winter 1984), in which he lists "five of the many cautions of which ministers in general, and pastoral counselors in particular, should be aware." These cautions are most appropriate in dealing with the depressed person or potential suicide.

First of all, the pastoral counselor should have a clear understanding of their role. He or she is not a substitute for the person's regular counselor, parish priest or spiritual director. The importance of making the proper referral is crucial when dealing with the depressed or suicide-prone person. Second, the pastoral counselor should not underestimate the complexity of a given situation. There is often a gap between the *stated* problem and the *real* problem. Third, the pastoral counselor needs to respect the uniqueness of each individual and not try to categorize each patient into a given "situation." The depressed or suicidal person will only become more so when we try to pigeonhole them. Fourth, the pastoral counselor needs a realistic view of human behavior. Human beings are a mixture of light and darkness. We need help in sorting our feelings and realizing our best possibilities. Finally, pastoral counselors should be clear about the "pastoral dimension" of their counseling. In other words, the pastoral counselor brings to the encounter a given religious story which seeks to highlight by faith the human dimensions of life. Pastoral counseling brings together this story and the life of the person in such a way that healing is possible. For example, we look at the person's depression or destructive desires in light of both the Christian story of God's unbounded love and the story of the person in conflict.

Dr. Cavanagh brings his article to a close with these words: "Pastoral counseling is not for amateurs or for professionals in related but different fields. Pastoral counseling is a serious endeavor, as serious as the practice of medicine or law; and some would even say that the stakes are infinitely higher." Yet we know that often individuals under stress do not go to professionals for help but turn to those near at hand—family and friends. What can we do to be of assistance when faced with the depressed or suicidal person?

Eugene Kennedy has been encouraging and enlightening many of us for some time with his thoughtful books on psychology and religion. Professor Kennedy has written a series of books on counseling for the non-professional who is called upon to render a type of emotional and even spiritual "first-aid." His books are balanced, prudent and Christian in the best sense of the term—the enhancement of our humanity to the praise of God. Kennedy addresses the problem of suicide in his excellent work, *On Becoming a Counselor.* The following are some good suggestions for effective counseling and helping by those who are non-professionals:

1. The distinction needs to be made between *attempted* and *completed* suicide. Special attention must be paid to attempted suicides by listening to what people are saying and *not* saying to us. Those who talk about suicide *do* commit suicide. The problem is that they are ignored or not taken seriously. The movement from vague thoughts to actual acts of self-destruction often follows a continuum with signals of tragedy evidenced along the way.

2. Kennedy records the following signs of suicidal attempts: increased stress, a lack of ability to cope, interpersonal crisis, loss of self-esteem, hopelessness, depression, disorientation, defiance, and a resentfulness that comes from being overly dependent on others. Also the high risk suicide victim is one who experiences little belonging to a meaningful community, tradition or system that bestows identity.

3. We should *avoid* over-reacting at all costs. There is a need for grace under pressure. Of course, we should be alert but not be an alarmist. Neither should we under-react and be so "supercool" that the person feels he or she must do something dramatic to prove they are serious to get our attention. Above all,

we should directly address the feelings of suicide and depression the person has experienced. Avoidance does no good. Provoking guilt feelings by appeals to religion or family seldom work and only heighten the feelings of self-hatred.

4. Total communication is crucial between the counselor and the suicidal person. Positive statements as well as statements about destruction must be faced head on. Let the person know that there are resources for positive living, and let them know their "suicidal-talk" has been heard by someone who cares. The counselor needs to explore his or her own feelings about suicide in order to find out how one will react (judgmental, fearful, controlling, accepting, etc.) to a suicidal person.

5. A person may encounter someone who has attempted suicide. Kennedy (drawing on the work of Hamilton and Moss, "Psychotherapy For the Suicidal Patient," in *Clues to Suicide*) outlines three stages in post-suicidal process: acute, convalescent and recovery. The acute phase is directed toward protection of the person from further harm. The convalescent phase occurs when the person is ready to return to his or her initial environment. The family is often in need of counseling and support at this time. The recovery phase calls for continued counseling and support so the person can deal effectively with feelings of frustration and self-hatred.

6. Finally, to be human is to be limited and finite. We cannot do everything for others. We need to realize that if a person strongly desires to commit suicide he or she can do so. The counselor must not make God-like demands on himself. To do so only decreases the counselor's effectiveness and increases his or her levels of guilt and anxiety. Counselors can do some very good and helpful things for those with suicidal tendencies. But counselors cannot do everything. Kennedy writes, "There are many good things counselors can do, but there are things they cannot achieve in the way of controlling the decisions of

others. The counselor's ability to balance these considerations determines their success in managing their own stress."

Suicide: A Spiritual Response

The parents of a person who had committed suicide shared with me the note he left: "Mom and Dad I love you. But I can't take the pain anymore." The pain of this young person was not of the physical sort but a pain that gripped the heart and stunted the soul. The pain that had become unbearable was the pain of existing but not being truly alive. The words of W.H. Auden come to mind: "Alive but alone, belong—where?—Unattached as tumbleweed" (*The Gift of Anxiety*). Too many people are lonely, unattached, and go through life as tumbleweed. They are searching for someone to care and listen—not to give answers or sound advice, but simply to stop and listen and hear the feelings that awkward words try to express. A wonderful little story told by Browne Barr captures this need.

A little girl was late in arriving home. Her father suffered a mixture of deep concern and purple anger at her disobedience. Finally she appeared coming up the road an hour late. The father was relieved that nothing had happened to her—at least not yet! He made sure she was fine and then have vent to his anger. "Why are you so late?", he demanded to know. The little girl explained that her friend had dropped her beautiful china doll and it broke into hundreds of pieces. The father's anger was cooled by the child's concern. "So you stayed with her to help pick up the pieces?" he said, his voice somewhat lower in tone. "No," said the young girl, "I stayed with Jane in order to help her cry."

What a beautiful answer! A real friend sometimes needs to stay with others in order to help them cry. There are times when we cannot put the pieces back together. The situation is too broken for our poor powers to make right. This does not mean that we are powerless. We can stay and help them in their grieving, even if we only help them to cry.

Not all the pains of life come from being alone and unattached (or even from china dolls). Our bed of pain can be physical, with the suffering coming from disease, illness or injury. We fear pain and loss of control. We fear the suffering which limits our freedom and narrows our world to the suffering itself. The elderly know a pain that comes from being our modern lepers—"obsolete"; "too slow"; "non-recyclable"; and "old" which itself is enough to consign one to the margins. When all is said, there is simply a fundamental pain that comes with being human. There is a basic flow and gap between what we are and what we are meant to be. What can we do?

The Christian vision and story are deeply challenged by the cries of the suffering. The Christian story holds that suffering (mental, physical or spiritual) is not a good in itself. We do not seek pain as an end. Death is never glorified or romanticized. Death, suffering and pain are disorders that we hope will be healed and made whole. The weakness of our human condition troubles us. We look for a *meaning*. Michael Quoist writes:

> Lord, suffering disturbs me, oppresses me.
> I don't understand why you allow it.
> Why, Lord?
> Why this innocent child who has been moaning for a week, horribly burned?
> This man who has been dying for three days and three nights, calling for his mother?
> This woman with cancer who in one month seems ten years older?
> This workman fallen from his scaffolding, a broken puppet less than twenty years old?

This stranger, poor isolated wreck, who is one great open sore?
This girl in a cast, lying on a board for more than thirty years?
Why Lord?
I don't understand.
Why this suffering in the world
that shocks,
isolates,
revolts,
shatters?
Why this hideous suffering that strikes blindly, seemingly without cause,
Falling unjustly on the good, and sparing the evil;
Which seems to withdraw, conquered by science, but comes back in another form, more powerful and more subtle?
I don't understand.
Suffering is odious and frightens me.
Why these people, Lord, and not others?
Why these, and not me?   (*Prayers*)

The Christian story does not promise that following Jesus will eliminate all pain, suffering and the certainty of death. What the Christian story does proclaim is that all these are transformed by the death and resurrection of Christ. Their *ultimate* victory has been denied by the new Adam who offers us the hope of sharing in his newness of life. Our sufferings and pain can be opportunities for us to draw closer to the crucified Jesus. René Latourelle, S.J. writes: "God, then has not eliminated suffering, but he has changed its meaning. When it is infused with love of the Innocent One who was crucified, it is illuminated from within. It transfigures, saves, divinizes . . . It is possible to conceive a world without suffering; but it is not possible to conceive of more love than is found in our suffering world" (*Man and His Problems in the Light of Jesus Christ*).

The God revealed by Jesus on the Cross is one who is totally involved in our human condition. The Cross reveals the depth of God's love for each of us. The prayer by Michael Quoist quoted above continues:

Son, it is not I, your God, who have willed suffering,
it is men.
They have brought it into the world in bringing sin,
Because sin is disorder, and disorder hurts.
There is for every sin, somewhere in the world and in time,
a corresponding suffering.
And the more sins there are, the more suffering.

But I came, and I took all your sufferings upon me,
as I took all your sins,
I took them and suffered them before you.
I transformed them, I made of them a treasure.
They are still an evil, but an evil with a purpose.
For through your sufferings, I accomplish Redemption.

(*Prayers*)

The Christian story does not offer us a catechism answer to suffering and death. The Bible does not come up with a set of "clear and distinct" ideas that will place the mind at rest. Rather, the stories of God counsel a different approach. We are offered the example of a life—the life of Jesus of Nazareth. The Word that becomes flesh is the word of suffering, enduring love. In this one life the brokenness of humanity is taken to Golgotha. The weakness and the folly of the Cross are to the eye of faith, the very power and wisdom of God. Father Latourelle, S.J. puts it so beautifully: "There is something more extravagant, something mightier than the power of evil; the seductive power of defenseless love. The response to the problem of evil is not refutation, but a figure, a person, a face tormented by suffering that is accepted with love."

The Christian story *continues* in history through the community of faith which proclaims that Jesus is Lord and which seeks to bring his healing love to all people. The Christian community actively seeks the brother and sister who is in special need of acceptance, forgiveness, comfort, consolation, hope, healing and Christ's unbounded love. The Christian community brings the power of love which tries to find an opening in the wall of pain which isolates. Love affirms the life of every person and offers hope for a new beginning. Even in the moments of our greatest pain and rejection, the Christian story challenges us to see the light that is already shining. In the midst of our dark nights we are asked to look for that new dawn and day. To those who are at the end of their powers to face life, the Christian story proclaims that at the very moment when all of our human powers are now powerless, the power of God shines through. When we feel we can endure no longer, the Spirit of God breathes new life in our souls.

The answer to those, young and old and all points and situations in between, who attempt suicide is love. Not just any love will do. It is the powerful love revealed on Golgotha; the love that allows for the hope of Easter; and the love that endures through brothers and sisters loving one another through Christ's name.

V

The Stewardship of Life

The Great Divide

Edd Doerr writes a column for *The Humanist* entitled, "Church and State." The March/April 1985 issue was devoted to the topic, "Abortion Rights." Mr. Doerr quoted with approval the following from Richard Critchfield:

> One might say that the great divide in the world today is not so much between the rich and the poor—or between the educated, healthier and wealthier and the illiterate, malnourished and impoverished—as between those who think that humans can shape their own destiny and those who still believe that one's fate is decided by outside forces.
>
> (*The Humanist*, March/April 1985)

Naturally Mr. Doerr and Mr. Critchfield raise their voices on behalf of those who believe that we can shape our own destiny. Man has been liberated from the superstition of religion and the bondage of tradition. Techno-scientific man has come of age and walks upright to face each new day. The only limits we face are self-imposed through our failure to use our intelligence and creativity to the full. However, in time we will overcome this as well. The kingdom of man will be realized with a paradise on earth. We need look no further than within our own resources of mind and spirit for the answers to big questions and for big solutions. We are free and not fated by the influence of the zodiac or the gods above. The heavens no longer proclaim the glory of God. The heavens, if they speak at all, simply remind us of our cosmic loneliness. Modern man is a combination of Prometheus and Adam. We have enormous knowledge and power. We have the fire that can destroy humankind. We have grasped at the tree of knowledge. What concerns us in our more sober moments is whether we have sufficient virtue for our knowledge and the will to choose life over death.

However, I do think Mr. Critchfield has put his pen on *the* modern question for humankind: do we claim to be self-masters, or do we accept our creaturehood in relation to a Creator? Yet this modern question is really a variation of the question which introduced our inquiry many pages ago. Namely, at this crossroad in history are we to choose life or death? To follow the God of Creation, Salvation and Re-creation is the way that leads to life in abundance. The covenant of life is the new covenant established through the death and resurrection of Jesus Christ. This covenant challenges us to accept our creatureliness and have the courage to stand before God in need. Such a covenant is not one of shame but of sharing—God sharing his very life with each of us in the Kingdom.

There is another road that can be traveled. It is well worn by the footprints of those who proclaim their own creation and redemption. This road is appealing because it gives the appearance that we are freely and maturely walking by our own light and with full responsibility. The tragedy lies in the failure to fully understand the tragedy of the human heart and history. Man is a limited, finite being whose history is a round of wheat and tares. Simply put: man cannot save himself, and history is the record that One was needed to enter history and humanity in order to effect such a healing. The Christian story proclaims this to have already taken place in the person of Jesus Christ. Furthermore, the Christian story goes even deeper in proclaiming that the human becomes fully human in Jesus. Apart from him we can never experience our true humanity. Father Richard A. McCormick, S.J. writes:

> It is the *human* that is then illumined by the person, teaching and achievement of Jesus Christ. The experience of Jesus is regarded as normative because he is believed to have experienced what it is to be *human* in the fullest way and at the deepest level. Christian ethics does not and cannot add to human ethical self-understanding as such any material content that is, in principle, strange or foreign to man as he exists and experiences himself.
>
> (*How Brave A New World?*)

In the preceding chapters we have discussed the three fundamental life issues that face us as a nation, a Church and as individuals. Abortion, euthanasia and suicide highlight our fundamental orientation towards life and the various ways we value human life. In addition, these issues reveal the fundamental story of our faith community. These issues expose to us the very nature of God, the expectations he has about how we treat one another, and the way we as Christians are called to be-in-the-world. Hence, the life-issues are much more than standard conversation for television or the "pick-me-ups" at a dull cocktail party. The way we tell our individual and community story concerning these issues reveals the deepest aspects of our moral character and identity.

In this last chapter we will address the following themes: Firstly, we shall explore the meaning and ways that we as Christians and as a faith community are called to be "counter-cultural." Secondly, we need to examine the preaching of Jesus and the centrality of the Kingdom of God. Our guide will be a familiar one—Stanley Hauerwas. Thirdly, we will offer a model of the Church (Dulles) which seriously addresses the life issues. And finally, we will bring our discussion to a close with a reflection on the dignity and sacredness of all human life. Naturally, such a closing is but an invitation for a new beginning.

Christ Transforming Culture

The now classic work by H. Richard Niebuhr, *Christ and Culture*, outlines a number of ways in which Christianity has related to culture. One of his typologies is Christ transforming culture. Such an approach or relationship involves the Christian story in a healthy tension with cultural values in which the culture is challenged to reflect the glory of God. Culture is not a demonic evil, but is in need of redemption and purification. The Church, or the faith community, does not try to destroy the culture, nor does she try to withdraw from the culture. The Church works with the culture in attempting to transform or change the culture so that human existence is respected and enhanced.

The transforming approach to culture is one that remains faithful to the vision of the Second Vatican Council and the witness of Scripture. The Second Vatican Council calls for a reading of the signs of the times and a willingness to honestly engage the questions of the modern world. We are to abandon the Catholic ghetto that characterized much of pre-Vatican II theology and Church life. Pope John XXIII and the Council Fathers challenged the people of God to bring the good news of salvation to a world in need of such news. Furthermore, the words of Jesus call for the Christian to remain in the world and bring God's healing love to all people. Such a view of the Church and her relation to the world is predominant in the Fourth Gospel: "I do not pray that you should take them out of the world, but that you should keep them from the evil one. They are not of the world, even as I am not of the world . . . As you sent me into the world, so I have sent them into the world. And for their sake I consecrate myself, that they also may be consecrated in truth" (Jn 17:15-16; 18-19). The disciples must remain in the world so that the news that Jesus is God's Son and that God is Love will be revealed throughout history. If the disciples were to withdraw from the world, this could not be done. Hence, it is a fundamental imperative that the Christian remain in, but not of, the world.

The Christian remains in the world and challenges the three (3) fundamental premises of modern culture: the will to power; technological culture and the reduction of the human person to a commodity; and emotivism as the way to make moral judgments. Let us examine each of these.

Will to power. A predominant theme of contemporary life is the will to dominate and control oneself and others. This will to power is based on the illusion that man is a self-creator and in need of no other. Man lives as if he is not finite and temporal. Anything or anyone which tries to reveal man's true condition must be overcome. Reinhold Niebuhr writes: "Man is ignorant and involved in the limitations of a finite mind: but he pretends that he is not limited. He assumes that he can gradually transcend finite limitations . . . All of his intellectual pursuits, therefore, become infected with the sin of pride. Man's pride and will to power disturb the harmony of creation . . . The ego which falsely makes itself the center of existence in its pride and will-to-power inevitably subordinates other life to its will and thus does injustice to other life" (*Nature and Destiny of Man*). In the phrase of M. Scott Peck, we become "the people of the lie." We live the untruth of our condition, namely, that we are not creatures beholding to a gracious God.

The Christian counsels not the will to power but the will to love. Not just any love is sufficient. The love that is stronger than any human willing or earthly power is the love of Jesus Christ. This is a love that calls the sinners, lepers, poor, sick, rejected, despised and unloved to sit and experience table-fellowship. The love of Jesus, and the love given to all who follow him, is one that seeks the lowest place; searches for the lost sheep; and washes the feet of others. The love of Jesus was perfected on Golgotha. The hour of Jesus' glory is the hour of his death. For it is on the Cross that the suffering love of God is revealed for all to see. The God who lives in unapproachable light; speaks from the whirl-wind; and then fills the Temple with his presence is the God who becomes flesh in Jesus and opens his arms to receive all who are in need of healing. The truth of God's love is consecrated through the love-sacrifice of Jesus.

Above all, the will to love comes to us first from the God who forgives, reconciles and binds up all our wounds. Stanley Hauerwas writes: "This love that is characteristic of God's kingdom is possible only for a forgiven people—a people who have learned not to fear one another" (*The Peaceable Kingdom*). Love drives out all fear. The will to power comes from a heart that is in the grip of fear and anxiety. At any moment someone or something may expose my vulnerability and weakness. My true condition would be seen and the illusion of my omnipotence would be shattered. In order to avoid the truth and live the lie, I must be in control and consume all who come within my influence.

Yet the will to love in imitation of Christ is the very willing-ness to be open to pain and to be moved by the suffering of others. St. Paul writes to the Corinthians: "If I must boast, I will boast of all the things that show my weakness" (2 Cor 11:30). Why? Because when we are weak, God can be strong in our lives. The weakest moment for Jesus, the Cross, is in reality the moment when he is strongest. For it is in the moment when his life was passing that true life was coming into the heart and history of all peoples. The love that Jesus reveals indicates that we need never fear to stand before God as we are. We are his creatures, his children, whom he loves eternally and unconditionally. God is oblivious to our status in the world. In fact, the more the world ignores the poor, the meek, the peacemakers, the pure, the children, the unborn, the dying and the suffering, the more all of these are heard by God. God's love is not something to be wrestled from him but a free gift to be received *and* shared with all his children.

Technological culture. The technological culture invites us to view the self, others, and all creation as commodities for consumption. Others are to be used in order to fulfill my desires. Others have a value only insofar as they are able to meet my wishes and can be used to advance my projects. When the others lose utility then they lose their value. In time, this marketing and consumption orientation turns the self into a thing or a commodity as well. John Francis Kavanaugh, S.J. writes:

> Marketing and consuming infiltrate every aspect of our lives and behavior. They filter all experience we have of ourselves. They become the standard of our final worth. Marketing and consuming ultimately reveal us to ourselves as things; and if we find ourselves revealed as things it will follow that our diverse capacities for knowledge are reduced to the truncated conditions of thing-like or commodity knowledge . . . What I am speaking of is a more subtle collapsing of human knowing into models and patterns which are more appropriate to cognition of things or commodities. (*Following Christ In A Consumer Culture*)

It follows that if we understand the self and others as nothing more than things or commodities, the ultimate norm or criterion for worth is utility or function. If the utility or function ceases, so does the value or reason for being. Hence, human life is seen as a thing that can be destroyed or kept according to one's will or utility. There is no inherent or alien dignity. The unborn can be aborted; the dying and suffering can be killed; and I can take my life when I find it too burdensome, since value and function are determined by me or by one more powerful.

Christianity tells the story of our humanity in a different way. Each human being is made in the image and likeness of God. There can be no reduction or denial of this sacredness and dignity. This is God's gift and presence in each person. The mightiest army or the wisest legislature cannot detract or add to human dignity. The person is created by God, redeemed by Christ, and renewed by the Spirit. Our individual story is intimately connected with the triune story of God. To the extent that we live our story in harmony with God's story, we fulfill our humanity and the dream God has for our life. By letting God's story be told through us we come to know joy, peace, happiness and a life that is Spirit-filled.

Furthermore, since life is a precious gift, we come to understand others as precious gifts of our gracious Father. The other is not a competition or a commodity. The other is a brother or sister of a common Father, Redeemer and Sanctifier. We are all members of a common family. The poorest of the poor; the weakest of the weak; the defenseless and the voiceless; the dying and the wretched of the earth all share a nobility and a dignity which cannot be destroyed. To love another person as Christ loves me (and them) is the minimum recognition of human dignity. John Wesley writes:

> A poor wretch cries to me for an alms: I look and see him covered with dirt and rags. But through these I see one that has an immortal spirit, made to know, and love, and dwell with God to eternity. I honor him for his Creator's sake. I see, through these rags, that he is purpled over with the blood of Christ. I love him for the sake of his Redeemer. The courtesy, therefore, which I feel and show toward him

is a mixture of the honor and love which I bear to the offspring of God; the purchase of His Son's blood, and the candidate for immortality.   ("On Pleasing All Men")

The other need not be feared or destroyed. The other, even though a stranger, may be an unexpected occasion for encountering God. Who is the stranger? Is it not the unborn and newly born; the neighbor next door as well as the co-worker; the family member and the dying loved one; and doesn't the stranger live within each of us? Is not the stranger who travels with us on our own road to Emmaus the hidden yet ever present Jesus? Edna McDonagh writes:

> The most threatening and rewarding aspect in human relationship is the constant re-emergence of the stranger. Someone as close as husband, wife, parent, child, lifelong friend, suddenly appears in an unexpected and unfamiliar guise . . . The stranger-friend is the model as well as the gateway to the totally transcendent God who is yet more intimate to me than I am to myself. Without the ability to rediscover the strangeness of God, faith languishes and theology is trivialized into the constant polishing of a petrified and domesticated idol. Autobiography as theology is about the search for the Perfect Stranger who comes to meet one in the imperfect strangers of daily life.
>
> (*Doing The Truth*)

Emotivism. One of the significant characteristics of the modern age is the loss of a common *telos* or goal for human existence. (Alasdair MacIntyre discusses this at length in his book, *After Virtue.*) This loss of a common *telos* or goal for daily living (guided by rational rules based on a common human nature) throws us into a highly individualized privatized and self-interested world. Each individual seeks his own goals (desires) and feels the need to overcome anyone or anything that stands in his way. All of this is morally acceptable since the goal is the fulfillment of one's desires. Any means can be used in order to accomplish this task. Our relationships become highly manipulative. We are free to use anyone and anything in order to satisfy our inner wants. If anyone disagrees with my goals or means it is just their opinion. Since there is no rational basis for morality, all moral judgments are based on the intensity of feeling, and there can be no argument as to right and wrong. The "argument" is settled through a contest of wills and by how many other wills we can assemble to support our feelings. Intensity of feeling becomes the litmus test for moral behavior. Sincerity is all that counts. It seldom occurs to ask if one can be sincerely wrong.

The Christian story (which includes the story of Israel) proclaims the good news that God wants to share his life with us. The story of God's unbounded love for us unites our various stories in one narrative lived to his praises. The fear and hostility of emotivism and the commodity mentality are replaced by love and communion with one another. When we allow God to tell his story through us, we experience that which unites us rather than that which divides. We share a common history, a common story, which helps us to see (vision) the world rightly. We see creation as a good gift from God. We see ourselves as finite, contingent beings made in the image and likeness of God. Above all, we are not separate individual selves, atoms or nomads motivated only by our feelings and desires. Rather, we are a community, a common people blessed with an uncommon God, that only comes to a proper self-understanding when we see the self *in relation* to others, creation and God.

Jesus and the Kingdom

The central message of the preaching of Jesus of Nazareth focuses on the Kingdom. "Reform your lives! The kingdom of heaven is at hand" (Mt 4:17). Nowhere does Jesus explain what the term "reign" or "kingdom" means. Jesus' disciples and audience were familiar with its meaning. However, this did not keep some of them from confusing the reign of God with an earthly, political kingdom. This is not what Jesus meant. Rather, *reign* or *kingdom* comes from the Greek word *basileia* which means an *act* of reigning rather than a geo-political entity. The reign of God is the active ruling of God as King in the lives, hearts and history of his people. The reign of God is his justice and righteousness experienced in the life of Israel and completed in the person of Jesus. In fact, Jesus is the Kingdom of God in the flesh. As Origen puts it, Jesus is the *autobasileia*.

The reign of God is found in the mighty deeds of God in Israel's history. The mightiest of deeds is Jesus. "Do not think that I have come to abolish the law and the prophets. I have come, not to abolish them, but to fulfill them" (Mt 5:17). The perfection of God's reign is experienced in the person of Jesus. The time of deliverance and healing is at hand. One must undergo a fundamental change of heart so as to be ready to respond. There can be no holding back or waiting for some later and more convenient hour. Now is the time when the reign of God is breaking into the world in a definitive and decisive way. The dead must bury their own and even the most intimate of relationships (wife and family) cannot stand in the way of the Kingdom.

To respond to Jesus and the Kingdom means that we live in the world, as individuals and as a community, in a new way. We are a Kingdom People on a journey toward God who is *here* and yet to come; present yet our Absolute Future. To lay everything aside to follow Jesus and the Kingdom requires that we pay the cost of discipleship. There can be no following of Jesus if we are not willing to undergo the death of change so as to be reborn into his likeness. There is no cheap grace. We cannot follow Jesus while holding on to the old order and securities. We must learn to live securely with insecurity. We leave our nets, boats, reputations and trophies in order to follow Jesus and see where he stays.

The cost of discipleship is not a lesson easily learned by modern man who wants to be in control and pull his own strings. The will to power, technological culture, and the imperial ego of emotivism rise up against a Kingdom of justice and peace and a Messiah who must suffer many things. The cost of discipleship demands that we acknowledge that this is God's world and we are part of his story. In being part of the Kingdom, we must love ourselves, deny ourselves, die to ourselves, and pick up our crosses daily. Many would rather have a Messiah and Kingdom of power, status and worldly authority. As Stanley Hauerwas writes:

> But Jesus then begins to tell them that he is not going to be recognized as having such power, but indeed will be rejected and killed. And Peter, still imbued with the old order, suggests this is no way for a savior to talk; saviors are people with power to affect the world. To save means to be 'in control" or to seek to be "in control," and Jesus seeks neither. His power is of a different order and the powers of this world will necessarily put him to death because they recognize, better than Peter, what a threat to power looks like. For here is one who invites others to participate in a kingdom of God's love, a kingdom which releases the power of giving and service. The powers of this world cannot comprehend such a kingdom. Here is a man who insists it is possible, if God's rule is acknowledged and trusted, to serve without power.   (*A Community of Character*)

The Kingdom of God not only changes hearts and visions but also allows for the establishment of a community of faith.

Kingdom people come together to share, witness and help transform the face of the earth. The new community of God's kingdom-story is one that offers a new way of existing in the world. The earthly kingdoms under the domination of Satan live by fear, manipulation, exploitation and violence. The Kingdom of God empowers people to live by love, trust, respect and peace. Through the way the Kingdom community lives a new world, a new creation, is slowly being revealed in human history. The old is passing away and the new is already shining.

The Kingdom of God and the community of faith stand in opposition to technological culture with its emphasis on power and machines, and to the self-understanding of man as creator. The Kingdom indicates that our life is a gift and that it only takes on meaning in relation to God. We need not engage in the fearful, frantic search for power and control. We do not have to hide from God because we are naked, vulnerable and in need. We can risk being seen as we are because God loves us as we are. Our true greatness does not come from machines, money, missiles or a rising GNP, but from the experience that we are sinners yet forgiven and accepted. The other (for example, the other who is a stranger in the womb) is to be welcomed as a gift and opportunity to encounter God. The life of the other (as well as my own) is to be reverenced. It is not a commodity to be used or a burden to be destroyed. Life is a trust to be lived in the truth that in weakness, strength reaches perfection.

To allow Jesus to become one's central story, and the Kingdom of God to be one's community, is to invite violence from the world. Jesus tells his disciples: "If the world hates you, know that it has hated me before it hated you. If you were of the world, the world would love its own; but because you are not of the world, therefore the world hates you. But I chose you out of the world" (Jn 15:18-19). To speak on behalf of the unborn, the sick, poor, suffering, dying and wretched of the earth is to disturb the "peace" and security of the comfortable. To make room for the stranger and keep fellowship with the suffering and dying challenges the mad dash for pleasure and ease. The principalities and powers of this world first try to ignore the Kingdom; then they ridicule as idealistic the belief that we can trust and love one another; and finally, the world turns to violence and death as a way of silencing those who dare speak and live God's story. Golgotha continues in human history.

Jesus not only told his disciples (and those who would continue to follow him) to expect opposition but he also indicated that he would not leave the community alone. "I will not leave you desolate; I will come to you" (Jn 14:18). The Paraclete will be sent to indwell within the heart of the disciple and the community. We need not fear what we are to say or how we are to act. The Paraclete will strengthen us at the hour of our trial. The power of the world is really weakness. Its wisdom is really foolishness. The use of violence brings about its own destruction. The Christian community exists in the world as the peaceable people who tell God's story. It is a story which proclaims that this is God's world, that our life is a gift, and that it is possible to love and care for one another. The Church dwells in a foreign land offering a vision of what life can be when we truly love one another as God first loved us.

Life-Church

The community that places the story of Jesus at the center of its life must exist in the world as a counter-sign and must challenge us to live life in abundance. The life-issues of abortion, euthanasia and suicide are not obsessive single issues but reveal our deepest values, our ways of relating to God, self and others, and the kind of world we are preparing to hand on to those who come after us. From the opening pages of scripture to its final book of hope (Revelation) the story of God is one of life. And the story of the God of life must continue to be told by the community that remains in the world. The mission of the Church is life. The ways in which the members of the Church relate to one another in love and trust, anticipate God's plan for his family. The way members of the faith community care for the unborn, weak, sick, lonely, poor and dying stand in opposition to the world's desire only for the strong. The Church offers a new way of existing. Stephen Charles Mott writes:

> Since the Bible shows our basic need for and dependence on community, it is not surprising that God's salvation calls us into community. The importance of the Church for salvation is not only that it is an instrument of God for our conversion, but also that what we are converted to is a new realm of social existence which God is calling into being . . . The Church, then, is a counter-community; alternating norms and values are organized into social groupings.
>
> *(Biblical Ethics and Social Change)*

The Christian community is one that "puts on Christ" and anticipates the new being, the new order, and the new creation. The Church is never to be identified totally with the Kingdom. This is triumphal idolatry. Rather, the Church is the first glimpse, a down payment, a signal of what it means to live God's story. The Church never does it perfectly. There is the stain of sin and the need for repentance and conversion within the Church. Yet she is entrusted with the good news of salvation, the news of God's forgiveness and healing love. By the way we relate to one another, we reveal what it means to tell God's story. St. Paul writes: "Therefore, as chosen and loved saints of God, put on a merciful heart, kindness, humility, gentleness, patience, bearing with one another and forgiving each other if anyone has a complaint against any other; . . . and in addition to all these put on love, which is the bond of completeness" (Col 3:12-14).

The community that tells the story of Yahweh-Jesus exhibits four marks: truth, justice, peace and joy. A word about each is in order.

Truth. The world—the lawless deeds and structures of humanity which stand in opposition to God—lives by lies and illusions. The world tells the story that human beings and this life are all there is. Man is the measure of all things. He is the creator and master of his fate. To be alive is to be in control and have the power to realize one's will. Anything or anyone who stands in our way must be overcome and conquered. Life is a commodity to be sold, used, exploited and discarded when it no longer serves any worldly function.

By contrast, the Christian story holds that this is God's world, that my life is a pure gift from a gracious God, and that the other is not a threat but an opportunity to encounter Jesus. The whole creation waits in anticipation and agony until the Lord comes again. Why? Simply because Jesus is Lord and all things are to be placed under his feet. We struggle in patient hope for that time when Jesus will be all in all. We never arrive at the point where we can say in truth. "I am complete by my own efforts. I have made it. I have written and told my own story apart from God or neighbor." This is the illusion and tragedy that blinds us to the truth that frees.

The truth that sets man free is nothing other than this: God loves us totally and unconditionally. We need not struggle, lie and mask our needs in order to appear strong or worthy. We need not abuse and neglect one another out of fear that we shall be overlooked or forgotten. The death and resurrection of Jesus Christ is our one hope of glory. Through the story of Jesus we become the children of God who are respected and loved into eternity. And because we are so loved we are empowered to love one another. We are to be one in love for God, self and neighbor.

Justice. Worldly justice is often understood as doing unto others *before* they do it to you. Even in our more enlightened moments we understand justice as the balancing of rights. Justice is the blindfolded Lady with scales balanced. The liberal view of justice (social contract) is one in which atomized individuals, motivated by self-interest, seek to maximize their outcome to the detriment of others. Society and its laws are merely in place to prevent violence and domestic unrest. Justice is rendering to each his due according to *merit*. One gets to own and use what one is entitled to based on personal achievement.

Biblical justice challenges the above and holds that human justice must reflect God's justice if it is to be authentic. That is, justice must be understood as generosity and the work of grace. Biblical justice is not based on merit but *need*. God responds to the *needs* of Israel and those who cry to him.

The divine response does not come because one has earned a hearing from God. Rather, God is a Just and Compassionate God who is attentive to the cry of the poor and the oppressed. The God of the Bible is an "affirmative action" God: he acts in behalf of those who have no one to plead their cause to. God does not give his love and gifts because we merit them; it is because we *need* them. In God's eyes it is acceptable to be needful. In fact, it is the recognition and acceptance of our needful condition that allows us to receive all that God has to give. Professor Mott writes:

> Biblical justice is biased in favor of the poor and the weak of the earth. This partiality was nowhere more clearly and succinctly stated than in the prophetic Beatitudes of Jesus: "Blessed are the poor . . . woe to the rich . . ." (Lk 20:20, 24). The first principle of justice in distribution is the correction of oppression. The poor are given priority only because their wretchedness requires greater attention if the equality called forth by the equal merit of all persons is to be achieved.   (*Biblical Ethics and Social Change*)

From the perspective of the Bible, there is no dichotomy between justice and love. Love is the foundation of justice and the meaning of the Law. In order to know what justice commands and the Law prescribes one must know what it is to love God and neighbor. Justice and laws give content to love in our interpersonal and institutional relationships. Justice is the active phase of love, and yet love always carries us beyond the demands of justice. Being obedient to the law and being a just person requires that one also possess a loving attitude. Love moves us to creatively respond to the needs of others without being told; often it means responding to the needs of others *in spite* of what we have been told or taught (the Good Samaritan, for example). Love allows us to see the enemy as a potential friend.

The justice and love which marks the Church as a people telling and living God's story makes a special place for the weak, sick, dying, unloved, vulnerable, voiceless and unborn. Special needs are recognized as making special claims on our power to love and reflect the generosity of God. For example, the unborn child comes to us vulnerable, in need and voiceless. The unborn are only "valued" if another values them. In themselves they contain no dignity or worth. Because of these negative conditions the Christian community must raise its voice and witness on their behalf. The Church holds that the unborn are loved by God in an unbounded way. There is no such thing as an "unwanted child." Every child is wanted and loved by God. The real poverty lies with us. The real tragedy is in our history. The real loss occurs in the heart that makes no room for this stranger. The same is true for the handicapped, elderly, depressed, sick and dying. The love and justice of the Church comes to expression in self-sacrifice and other-remembering.

Peace. The fruit of justice is peace. For there can be no true and lasting peace without justice. If we do not live in right-relationship with God, self, neighbor and nature we cannot experience peace. We may have the illusion of peace—that is, a quietism that does not disturb our comfort and ease. But this is not the kind of peace that God wants us to know. Worldly peace is often understood as the absence of conflict or a non-involvement with others that counsels "a live and let live attitude." However, "live and let live" is often experienced as "live and let die." For when we refuse to get involved in the lives of others and in the great issues of the day, all in the name of tolerance and civility, we deny others our gifts and insights. Non-involvement is a form of violence and death. The rich man in the parable (Lk 16:19-31) did not directly hurt Lazarus. He simply ignored him. The rich man was preoccupied with feasting and luxury. The dogs were more attentive to the needs of Lazarus since they licked his sores. The rich man could only hear the request of his guests for more food, drink and music. The rich man was left undisturbed by Lazarus but he did not know true peace.

The Church, the community of faith that tells and lives by the story of Jesus Christ, must be a community of peace. At the center of our peacemaking is the virtue of patience. The peacemaking Church refuses to pick up the sword of instant results and quick fixes. The Church must learn to be patient as God is patient. We work for changes in our society but we do so without appealing to the methods of earthly principalities and powers. The peace Church exists in a world of violence and challenges that violence. We are called to speak truth to power in the name of justice and love. To be specific, we challenge the fundamental lie of worldly existence which holds that we humans are in control and are the ultimate masters of our fate. The peace Church proclaims our dependence upon God and that all of reality finds its true meaning in his story. Naturally, the response of the world is predictable—violence and death.

The Church of peace has her vision fixed on the weak and the defenseless. She continues to search for Lazarus in our midst. Lazarus is the beggar on our urban streets and the bag lady who moves from doorway to doorway. Lazarus is the unborn whom the world fails to recognize as "a person in the full Constitutional sense of the term." Lazarus is the sick and the dying and the elderly who do not make a significant contribution to society. Lazarus comes to us in the handicapped and the mentally ill who desperately seek compassion and love. We want peace and we try to secure it by missiles, a rising GNP, more technology and by extolling the "life styles of the rich and famous." Yet the peace of the world is an illusion. True peace comes when we recognize a brother or sister in the unborn, handicapped, elderly, sick, dying and rejected. In other words, it is in the stranger whom the world calls a threat that the peace Church welcomes as a gift. And what is even more shocking, the peace Church welcomes the stranger as the hidden, needful presence of Jesus Christ.

Joy. Pleasure is often confused with joy. In a culture which seeks ease and comfort, this is not surprising. We are "happy" when we have our "creature wants" met. The focus of pleasure is the imperial self. Joy is the satisfaction of desires which give pleasure to the self. Such joy, pleasure and happiness are very short lived since they focus totally on the sensate level of our humanity. Professor of Philosophy Peter J. Kreeft has written a delightful book entitled, *Heaven, The Heart's Deepest Longing*. In his extended discussion of joy Kreeft writes:

> In ek-static joy we forget ourselves. But we also forget joy, for joy points beyond joy to its object, to God. This precisely *is* its joy, its ek-statis. Joy can no more be caught than the wind. We are swept up in joy's heavenly hurricane. It is not the goal but the vehicle, Elijah's fiery chariot.
>
> Joy is so fascinating that it is easy to forget this and make joy itself the goal . . . Joy is the touch of God's finger. The object of our longing is not the touch but the Toucher. This

is true of all good things—they are all God's touch. Whatever we desire, we are really desiring of God.

True joy carries us beyond the cravings of the imperial ego and
the illusion of self-sufficiency. Joy dispels the fears and violence
that must be employed in telling our story apart from God. Joy
frees us to live in this passing world with our hearts set on the
one that lasts forever. Just before he died, Jesus told his disciples
that they need not be anxious or fearful. Their sadness and
weeping will be turned to joy—but not the joy of the world
whose story is built on illusions and lies. Jesus comes to bring a
joy the world cannot give or take away—a joy that assures us of
acceptance, forgiveness and unbounded love. Joy comes to the
heart and Church that experience God's healing love. The
Church which tells and lives the story of Jesus is one "surprised
by joy." Why? Because we find out that we can face life without
the need to control and dominate. We can surrender to God and
find that such a surrender is our real fulfillment.

   The Church of Jesus Christ proclaims the truth; relates by
justice and love; labors for peace; and knows how to live joyfully.
For the Church that tells the story of Jesus must make welcome
the stranger. The stranger is a gift who constantly surprises us
with new gifts, insights and opportunities to encounter God. We
are surprised by joy because we learn how much the stranger
(unborn, newborn, elderly, handicapped, sick and dying) en-
larges our capacity for generous love. Husbands and wives truly
know what marital love is with the arrival of the stranger we call
a child. Friends know the price of love when they remain in
solidarity with the sick and dying. Those who are isolated and
troubled by mental illness need someone to simply care. In the
midst of life and death we are a people of joy because we know
that in life and death and beyond we belong to the Lord.

The Stewardship of Life

We introduced our reflections on the life issues by recounting the story of our ancestors in faith in the wilderness. The Israelites stood at the crossroads between life and death. Today, modern man finds himself at a similar juncture. One road leads to God and eternal life. Another path leads to destruction and death. Our choice depends a great deal on how we value human life and how we understand life—as a gift or as a possession. Furthermore, life issues highlight the ways we treat the stranger and make room in our heart and lives for the weak and dying. Our reflections on abortion, euthanasia and suicide are offered from the perspective of Jesus' story as the authentic way of respecting life. Jesus' story tells us that each person is a son or daughter of a gracious God who desires to share his life with us. This gracious God makes a special place in his Kingdom for the uninvited of this world. The least of our brethren are the honored guests.

Paddy Chayefsky wrote a famous play entitled *Gideon*. It is the powerful story of the encounter between God and man. God uses Gideon to defeat the ten thousand Midianites. However, Gideon is tempted to claim God's victory as his own. Chayefsky offers the following dialogue between Abimelech, Gideon and the angel of God:

Abimelech: "We all wait to hear you tell the miracle of God's victory over Midian."

Gideon: "A miracle? Why do you call it that? My, my uncles, the war with Midian was not mysterious, but only the inevitable outgrowth of historico-economic, socio-psychological and cultural forces prevailing in these regions."

The Angel: "Oh it is amusing.
God no more believes it odd
That man does not believe in God,
Man believes the best he can
Which means, it seems, belief in man.
Then let him don my golden ephod
And let him be a proper God.
Well, let him try it anyway
With this conceit, we end the play."

The play may be ended with this conceit but the temptation to claim God's victories as our own continues. Techno-biological man is swollen with the pride that comes from the work of his hands. The ultimate conceit is for man to replace God as the master and author of all reality. Kenneth Vaux writes:

> Man is become like God. He possesses power to give and take life. In the Greek sense he has stolen knowledge, fire and hope (insight, energy and foresight) from the gods and now must learn to live responsibly with these powers. The history of his consciousness is marked with a religious perception and a humanistic urge. He has experienced the divine power as savior and judge, possibility and limitation. From pagan mythology he has been tantalized with the possibility of the death of God, the *Götterdämmerung* where the gods execute themselves out of being so that man can and must become God.   (*Bio-medical Ethics*)

Yet man is not God. Man is called to be a part—a special part, but a part nonetheless—of God's story for creation. Man is a creature who is finite, limited, temporal, and will ultimately die. However, man's death sentence is not a cause of despair and resignation. Man's death sentence has been commuted and transformed by the death and resurrection of Christ. Man is meant for glory. Not the glory of his works and this world, but the glory that comes as pure gift from God.

We have spoken a great deal about life in these pages. The responsibility and opportunity for witnessing to God's gift and enhancing that gift is great. The power and bravado of the technological culture is being seriously questioned. The mushroom cloud and the acid rain are reminders that the gadgets of our world do not come cheaply or without the need for critical evaluation. Many today are searching for a good news that offers a better way. People today are searching for the good news of life in abundance. And isn't that what the Church of Jesus Christ is about? As Karl Barth reminds us, the Church must be "to the world of men around it a reminder of the law of the kingdom of God already set up on earth in Jesus Christ, and a promise of its future manifestation . . . there is already on earth an order which is based on the great alteration of the human situation and directed towards its manifestation" (*Church Dogmatics*).

The depth of our love and commitment to the unborn, the dying and the despondent reveals to a world of violence a new way of existing. The future of God's Kingdom is revealed, however briefly, in the now of our everydayness. When we cherish the special ones of God the Kingdom comes a little closer and God's will is done in heaven and on earth.

Case Studies

One way to approach the study of bio-medical ethics is by using the case-method. Cases are constructed for consideration which highlight various values in conflict and medical-moral issues which often go undetected. While this method has much to commend it (see the excellent book by Robert M. Veatch, *Case Studies in Medical Ethics*), there are also drawbacks. Chief among them is the false belief that medical ethics is merely problem solving. Such an approach often neglects the "human factor." That is, in solving case problems we can overlook the need to form a virtuous character in the physician and the need to treat the patient as a unique person. Education in biomedical ethics must never forget a fundamental goal: to develop in the physician a moral character as powerful as the knowledge he possesses. With that in mind, we offer the following three cases dealing with the life issues of abortion, euthanasia and suicide.

Abortion: Can you have it all?

Jane and Bob are happily married with no children—yet. Both are professionals and are practicing Roman Catholics. They could be called in the current vernacular "yuppies" (Young Urban Professionals). To be specific, Bob is a young lawyer and Jane has an "exciting and challenging" job with a large investment company. During the past two years she has made steady progress and is now beginning to manage some of the firm's larger accounts.

During a routine visit to her physician, Jane received the news that she had suspected but hoped was not true. She was pregnant. To put the matter as politely as one can—this was an unplanned pregnancy. Jane was shocked and angered. She did not want *this* pregnancy at *this* time. Things were going so well with her marriage and her job—and now this. What would Bob say?

At dinner that evening (she did her best to hide the news initially) she told Bob she was pregnant. Bob was overjoyed with the news. He would be a father. As he talked and showed signs of affection to Jane, he suddenly caught himself. She was unresponsive except for a misty look in her eyes which he initially took for joy. Now he realized it was sadness. Jane finally said, "Bob, I am not sure I want this baby now." The joy came to a sudden stop. Jane wanted to discuss options.

Bob immediately panicked and became angry. Abortion was out of the question. Yet it was not out of the question for Jane. She told Bob she had rights and feelings as well. It would be she who would have to carry the baby. She would have to interrupt her career and stay home. If she had a sitter or daycare she would feel guilty about not properly providing for the child. It was easy for Bob to be happy. He "suffered" none of the consequences.

Bob began to doubt his position. Maybe he was being unrealistic. Maybe he wasn't listening enough to Jane's needs. After all, this is a new day and a new way of understanding pregnancy, family and the role of women. The more he thought, he more confused he became. Finally, he suggested they go see Father James at the parish. Jane respected him and liked him as a friend. Even so, she was reluctant but finally agreed.

* How would you describe the attitudes of Bob and Jane toward marriage, each other and the place of children in a marriage?
* Do you think Jane and Bob's reaction to the news of pregnancy is typical of today? Is it becoming more common? Why is this so? What are the benefits and the liabilities of such changes in attitudes on these sensitive issues?
* If you were Father James, how would you handle this case?
* If you were a friend of Bob and Jane, what advice would you give?

Euthanasia: Do No Harm?

Dr. Phillips is a dedicated and caring physician. Most of his work is with those dying of cancer. His special interest is the elderly who suffer the pain of cancer and are approaching the end of life. Dr. Phillips is concerned about more than pain management. He wants to always respect the sacredness of life.

One patient, Alice Stewart, has become special to Dr. Phillips. She is a fighter. For the past few months, Alice has suffered from terminal cancer and has been under the care of Dr. Phillips. She has been an inspiration. She seldom complains, and accepts all that she receives as an opportunity to grow in love of God. One day after she had an especially painful night (and a bad week as a whole), Dr. Phillips could see that all was not well. He probed further. Finally she said with a rush of tears, "I can't take it any more. Please help me to die faster and without this pain."

Dr. Phillips was deeply shaken. Could this be his fighter and grand lady? Where was her courage and faith. Alice was asking him to do something that was contrary to everything he had been taught, believed and had fought against. Yet if Alice could make such a request, he must seek some answers. For if a woman of such inspiration could turn to a different course, could there be a time when it is not harmful to kill and when it may be merciful to directly end this useless pain?

* How would you analyze Ms. Stewart's "sudden" change of attitude?
* What advice would you offer to Dr. Phillips and Ms. Stewart? What spiritual direction could be offered to Ms. Stewart in light of her sufferings?
* In what ways could Ms. Stewart's family and friends be an important form of support? How can her parish community provide spiritual and faith resources?

Suicide: The Civilized Thing To Do?

Alice and Jeffrey have been married for twenty-eight years. They have one grown daughter who is happily married and lives in another city. Alice has been ill for some time and Jeffrey spends most of his free time looking after her needs in their comfortable townhouse. Jeffrey is a writer and a professor at the local university. They love each other very much. In fact, both indicate that their love has been deepened by Alice's illness.

One day after a series of classes and some early morning writing, Jeffrey found Alice alone in her darkened room. He became concerned and asked her what she was doing. She told him not to worry. She was only doing some serious thinking after a recent visit to her physician.

Dr. Jacobs had indicated that Alice's illness was about to move into its final phase. Her appetite would lessen. She would experience a loss of memory and disconcerting changes in moods. She would go through periods of intense activity and then fall into a pattern of prolonged sleep. Finally, she would be confined to bed and eventually die. The pain to her head and face would be quite severe.

Jeffrey assured Alice that she need not worry. He would stay with her to the end. He loved her very much. Alice replied that she knew of his love. But that was not the issue. She wanted to commit suicide so as to avoid such a fate and spare Jeffrey the pain of watching and caring for her in this last phase. Suicide offered both dignity and mercy.

* How would you respond if you were Jeffrey? Suppose you were the daughter?
* What spiritual direction could be offered to Alice and Jeffrey? What views of life, suffering, marital love and death seem to be held by this couple?
* Are there instances when suicide is rational and civilized? Why can't we take our life if there is only pain and suffering in the future? Isn't this a genuine way of sparing our loved ones the pain of seeing us this way?

Note: The above cases and questions are kept short and many details are intentionally omitted. We hope this will allow the reader more freedom to supply details and approach these cases from a number of different perspectives depending upon various added details. Naturally, these cases are fictitious and any similarity to any person living or dead is a mere coincidence.

Declaration on Euthanasia

Vatican Congregation for the Doctrine of the Faith
June 26, 1980

Introduction

The rights and values pertaining to the human person occupy an important place among the questions discussed today. In this regard, the Second Vatican Ecumenical Council solemnly reaffirmed the lofty dignity of the human person, and in a special way his or her right to life. The council therefore condemned crimes against life "such as any type of murder, genocide, abortion, euthanasia or willful suicide" (Pastoral Constitution, *"Gaudium et Spes"* no. 27).

More recently, the Sacred Congregation for the Doctrine of the Faith has reminded all the faithful of Catholic teaching on procured abortion. The congregation now considers it opportune to set forth the Church's teaching on euthanasia.

It is indeed true that, in this sphere of teaching, the recent popes have explained the principles, and these retain their full force, but the progress of medical science in recent years has brought to the fore new aspects of the question of euthanasia, and these aspects call for further elucidation on the ethical level.

In modern society, in which even the fundamental values of human life are often called into question, cultural change exercises an influence upon the way of looking at suffering and death;

moreover, medicine has increased its capacity to cure and to prolong life in particular circumstances, which sometimes give rise to moral problems.

Thus people living in this situation experience no little anxiety about the meaning of advanced old age and death. They also begin to wonder whether they have the right to obtain for themselves or their fellowmen an "easy death," which would shorten suffering and which seems to them more in harmony with human dignity.

A number of episcopal conferences have raised questions on this subject with the Sacred Congregation for the Doctrine of the Faith. The congregation, having sought the opinion of experts on the various aspects of euthanasia, now wishes to respond to the bishops' questions with the present declaration, in order to help them to give correct teaching to the faithful entrusted to their care, and to offer them elements for reflection that they can present to the civil authorities with regard to this very serious matter.

The considerations set forth in the present document concern in the first place all those who place their faith and hope in Christ, who, through his life, death and resurrection, has given a new meaning to existence and especially to the death of the Christian, as St. Paul says: "If we live, we live to the Lord, and if we die, we die to the Lord" (Romans 14:8; cf. Philippians 1:20).

As for those who profess other religions, many will agree with us that faith in God the creator, provider and Lord of life—if they share this belief—confers a lofty dignity upon every human person and guarantees respect for him or her.

It is hoped that this declaration will meet with the approval of many people of good will, who philosophical or ideological differences notwithstanding, have nevertheless a lively awareness of the rights of the human person. These rights have often in fact been proclaimed in recent years through declarations issued by international congresses, and since it is a question here of fundamental rights inherent in every human person, it is obviously wrong to have recourse to arguments from political pluralism or religious freedom in order to deny the universal value of those rights.

I. The Value of Human Life

— Human life is the basis of all goods, and is the necessary source and condition of every human activity and of all society. Most people regard life as something sacred and hold that no one may dispose of it at will, but believers see in life something greater, namely a gift of God's love, which they are called upon to preserve and make fruitful. And it is this latter consideration that gives rise to the following consequences:

1. No one can make an attempt on the life of an innocent person without opposing God's love for that person, without violating a fundamental right, and therefore without committing a crime of the utmost gravity.

2. Everyone has the duty to lead his or her life in accordance with God's plan. That life is entrusted to the individual as a good that must bear fruit already here on earth, but that finds its full perfection only in eternal life.

3. Intentionally causing one's own death, or suicide, is therefore equally as wrong as murder; such an action on the part of a person is to be considered as a rejection of God's sovereignty and loving plan. Furthermore, suicide is also often a refusal of love for self, the denial of the natural instinct to live, a flight from the duties of justice and charity owed to one's neighbor, to various communities or to the whole of society—although, as is generally recognized, at times there are psychological factors present that can diminish responsibility or even completely remove it.

However, one must clearly distinguish suicide from that sacrifice of one's life whereby for a higher cause, such as God's glory, the salvation of souls or the service of one's brethren, a person offers his or her own life or puts it in danger (cf. John 15:14).

II. Euthanasia

In order that the question of euthanasia can be properly dealt with, it is first necessary to define the words used.

Etymologically speaking, in ancient times euthanasia meant an easy death without severe suffering. Today one no longer thinks of this original meaning of the word, but rather of some intervention of medicine whereby the sufferings of sickness or of the final agony are reduced, sometimes also with the danger of suppressing life prematurely. Ultimately, the word euthanasia is used in a more particular sense to mean "mercy killing," for the purpose of putting an end to extreme suffering, or saving abnormal babies, the mentally ill or the incurably sick from the prolongation, perhaps for many years, of a miserable life, which could impose too heavy a burden on their families or on society.

It is therefore necessary to state clearly in what sense the word is used in the present document.

By euthanasia is understood an action or an omission which of itself or by intention causes death, in order that all suffering may in this way be eliminated. Euthanasia's terms of reference, therefore, are to be found in the intention of the will and in the methods used.

It is necessary to state firmly once more that nothing and no one can in any way permit the killing of an innocent human being, whether a fetus or an embryo, an infant or an adult, an old person, or one suffering from an incurable disease, or a person who is dying. Furthermore, no one is permitted to ask for this act of killing, either for himself or herself or for another person entrusted to his or her care, nor can he or she consent to it, either explicitly or implicitly. Nor can any authority legitimately recommend or permit such an action. For it is a question of the violation of the divine law, an offense against the dignity of the human person, a crime against life, and an attack on humanity.

It may happen that, by reason of prolonged and barely tolerable pain, for deeply personal or other reasons, people may be led to believe that they can legitimately ask for death or obtain it for others. Although in these cases the guilt of the individual may be reduced or completely absent, nevertheless the error of judgment into which the conscience falls, perhaps in good faith, does not change the nature of this act of killing, which will always be in itself something to be rejected.

The pleas of gravely ill people who sometimes ask for death are not to be understood as implying a true desire for euthanasia; in fact it is almost always a case of an anguished plea for help and love. What a sick person needs, besides medical care, is love, the human and supernatural warmth with which the sick person can and ought to be surrounded by all those close to him or her, parents and children, doctors and nurses.

III. The Meaning of Suffering for Christians and the Use of Painkillers

Death does not always come in dramatic circumstances after barely tolerable sufferings. Nor do we have to think only of extreme cases. Numerous testimonies which confirm one another lead one to the conclusion that nature itself has made provision to render more bearable at the moment of death separations that would be terribly painful to a person in full health. Hence it is that a prolonged illness, advanced old age, or a state of loneliness or neglect can bring about psychological conditions that facilitate the acceptance of death.

Nevertheless the fact remains that death, often preceded or

accompanied by severe and prolonged suffering, is something which naturally causes people anguish.

Physical suffering is certainly an unavoidable element of the human condition; on the biological level, it constitutes a warning of which no one denies the usefulness; but, since it affects the human psychological makeup, it often exceeds its own biological usefulness and so can become so severe as to cause the desire to remove it at any cost.

According to Christian teaching, however, suffering, especially suffering during the last moments of life, has a special place in God's saving plan; it is in fact a sharing in Christ's Passion and a union with the redeeming sacrifice which he offered in obedience to the Father's will. Therefore one must not be surprised if some Christians prefer to moderate their use of painkillers, in order to accept voluntarily at least a part of their sufferings and thus associate themselves in a conscious way with the sufferings of Christ crucified (cf. Matthew 27:34).

Nevertheless it would be imprudent to impose a heroic way of acting as a general rule. On the contrary, human and Christian prudence suggest for the majority of sick people the use of medicines capable of alleviating or suppressing pain, even though these may cause as a secondary effect semi-consciousness and reduced lucidity. As for those who are not in a state to express themselves, one can reasonably presume that they wish to take these painkillers, and have them administered according to the doctor's advice.

But the intensive use of painkillers is not without difficulties, because the phenomenon of habituation generally makes it necessary to increase their dosage in order to maintain their efficacy. At this point it is fitting to recall a declaration by Pius XII, which retains its full force; in answer to a group of doctors who had put the question: "Is the suppression of pain and consciousness by the use of narcotics—permitted by religion and morality to the doctor and the patient (even at the approach of death and if one foresees that the use of narcotics will shorten life)?"

The Pope said: "If no other means exist, and if, in the given circumstances, this does not prevent the carrying out of other religious and moral duties: Yes." In this case, of course, death is in no way intended or sought, even if the risk of it is reasonably taken; the intention is simply to relieve pain effectively, using for this purpose painkillers available to medicine.

However, painkillers that cause unconsciousness need special consideration. For a person not only has to be able to satisfy his or her moral duties and family obligations; he or she also has to prepare himself or herself with full consciousness for meeting Christ. Thus Pius XII warns: "It is not right to deprive the dying person of consciousness without a serious reason."

IV. Due Proportion in the Use of Remedies

Today it is very important to protect, at the moment of death, both the dignity of the human person and the Christian concept of life, against a technological attitude that threatens to become an abuse. Thus, some people speak of a "right to die," which is an expression that does not mean the right to procure death either by one's own hand or by means of someone else, as one pleases, but rather the right to die peacefully with human and Christian dignity. From this point of view, the use of therapeutic means can sometimes pose problems.

In numerous cases, the complexity of the situation can be such as to cause doubts about the way ethical principles should be applied. In the final analysis, it pertains to the conscience either of the sick person, or of those qualified to speak in the sick person's name, or of the doctors, to decide, in the light of moral obligations and of the various aspects of the case.

Everyone has the duty to care for his or her own health or to seek such care from others. Those whose task it is to care for the sick must do so conscientiously and administer the remedies that seem necessary or useful.

However, is it necessary in all circumstances to have recourse to all possible remedies?

In the past, moralists replied that one is never obliged to use "extraordinary" means. This reply, which as a principle still holds good, is perhaps less clear today, by reason of the imprecision of the term and the rapid progress made in the treatment of sickness. Thus some people prefer to speak of "proportionate" and "disproportionate" means.

In any case, it will be possible to make a correct judgment as to the means by studying the type of treatment to be used, its degree of complexity or risk, its cost and the possibilities of using it, and comparing these elements with the results that can be expected, taking into account the state of the sick person and his or her physical and moral resources.

In order to facilitate the application of these general principles, the following clarifications can be added:

— If there are no other sufficient remedies, it is permitted with the patient's consent, to have recourse to the means provided by the most advanced medical techniques, even if these means are still at the experimental stage and are not without a certain risk. By accepting them, the patient can even show generosity in the service of humanity.

— It is also permitted, with the patient's consent, to interrupt these means, where the results fall short of expectations. But for such a decision to be made, account will have to be taken of the reasonable wishes of the patient's family, as also of the advice of the doctors who are specially competent in the matter. The latter may in particular judge that the investment in instruments and personnel is disproportionate to the results foreseen; they may also judge that the techniques applied impose on the patient strain or suffering out of proportion with the benefits which he or she may gain from such techniques.

— It is also permissible to make do with the normal means that medicine can offer. Therefore one cannot impose on anyone the obligation to have recourse to a technique which is already in use but which carries a risk or is burdensome. Such a refusal is not the equivalent of suicide; on the contrary, it should be considered as an acceptance of the human condition, or a wish to avoid the application of a medical procedure disproportionate to the results that can be expected, or a desire not to impose excessive expense on the family or the community.

— When inevitable death is imminent in spite of the means used, it is permitted in conscience to take the decision to refuse forms of treatment that would only secure a precarious and burdensome prolongation of life, so long as the normal care due to the sick person in similar cases is not interrupted. In such circumstances the doctor has no reason to reproach himself with failing to help the person in danger.

Conclusion

The norms contained in the present declaration are inspired by a profound desire to serve people in accordance with the plan of the creator. Life is a gift of God, and, on the other hand, death is unavoidable; it is necessary therefore that we, without in any way hastening the hour of death, should be able to accept it with full responsibility and dignity. It is true that death marks the end of our earthly existence, but at the same time it opens the door to immortal life. Therefore all must prepare themselves for this event in the light of human values, and Christians even more so in the light of faith.

As for those who work in the medical profession, they ought

to neglect no means of making all their skill available to the sick and the dying; but they should also remember how much more necessary it is to provide them with the comfort of boundless kindness and heartfelt charity. Such service to people is also service to Christ the Lord, who said: "As you did it to one of the least of these my brethren, you did it to me" (Matthew 25:40).

At the audience granted to the undersigned prefect, His Holiness Pope John Paul II approved this declaration, adopted at the ordinary meeting of the Sacred Congregation for the Doctrine of the Faith, and ordered its publication.

Rome, the Sacred Congregation for the Doctrine of the Faith, 5 May 1980.

> *Franjo card. Seper*
> *Prefect*
> *Jerome Hamer, O.P.*
> *Tit. Archbishop of Lorium, secretary*

(Origins 10 (1980): 154-57.)

Consistent Ethic of Life:
"Morally Correct, Tactically Necessary"

"I am convinced that demonstrating the linkage between abortion and other issues is both morally correct and tactically necessary for the pro-life position that I have been addressing," Cardinal Joseph Bernardin said June 7 in remarks to the National Right to Life Convention in Kansas City, Mo. Bernardin, chairman of the U.S. bishops' pro-life activities committee, was referring to the consistent ethic on life issues that he proposed in an address at Fordham University in December 1983 (Origins, vol. 13, pp. 491ff) and at St. Louis University in April 1984 (Origins, vol. 13, pp. 705ff). In Kansas City, Bernardin said: "In working to change national policy on abortion, I submit that we must cast our case in broadly defined terms, in a way which elicits support from others. We need to shape our position consciously in a way designed to generate interest in the abortion question from individuals who thus far have not been touched by our witness or our arguments." His text follows.

I first wish to express my appreciation for the opportunity to address this convention of the National Right to Life Committee. I take the chairmanship of the National Conference of Catholic Bishops Committee for Pro-Life Activities as a very serious responsibility and a significant opportunity for service. I am convinced of the total personal commitment of each of our bishops to the philosophy and program of the pro-life movement. I am also equally convinced that the heart and soul of the movement is the personal dedication of all those who are represented at this meeting.

I thought it might be most useful for me to set forth in this address a general perspective of where we stand in the struggle against abortion, the struggle to protect the life of the unborn. It is now 11 years since the Supreme Court decisions which legalized abortion on request; there are lessons to be learned from this decade. In light of this experience, we can also establish our future direction.

The Past: Witness for Life

An examination of the past decade generates both sadness and pride. Sadness—perhaps moral dismay is a better phrase—is a product of evaluating the abortion policy set in place by the 1973 Supreme Court decisions. Pride is the justifiable product of evaluating the efforts of thousands of volunteers who are committed to reversing the present national policy and establishing respect for the right to life as a national policy and practice.

First, the implications of *Roe v. Wade* bear examination. In order to grasp the dimensions of the present challenge we face, it is necessary to describe the depth of the problem created by the 1973 Supreme Court decisions. The decisions were radical in nature and systematic in their consequences. They were radical since they overturned in one stroke an existing political and legal structure which treated any form of abortion as an exception to normal practice. The end product of *Roe v. Wade* was to establish a political and legal framework with no restraint on abortion. Many of us sensed then, and all of us can be sure now, that public opinion was not at all in favor of a policy opening the floodgates to 1.5 million abortions a year. Some radical decisions are justified morally and they are necessary politically, but the court decisions of 1973 were neither justified, necessary nor acceptable to large segments of the American public.

The court's decisions were systematic in the sense that they changed not only a given law, but they established operating presumptions in medical practice, social service agencies and administrative policy which legitimated and facilitated access to abortion. The result of the decisions was to change the structure of this society's approach to abortion. What the decisions did not change was the substantial, broad-based and solidly grounded view of American citizens across the land that abortion on request is not a satisfactory way to address the real problem individuals and families face in this delicate area of respecting unborn life.

It was this deeply felt personal opposition to abortion which crystallized the public-policy position of the pro-life movement. There has undoubtedly been a strong Catholic core to this movement, but it has cut across religious and political lines, as is evidenced by the participants in this convention. It is this pro-life constituency which is an authentic source of pride for anyone associated with it. At a time when grass-roots coalitions are often talked about, the pro-life constituency has a claim second to none in demonstrating local support. At a time when citizen apathy is a serious public problem, the pro-life movement has mobilized men and women personally, professionally and politically in opposition to abortion. At a time when the moral dimension of public policy on a variety of issues is in need of a clear statement, the pro-life movement has cast the political issue in decisively moral terms. Finally, the movement has been not only political but pastoral. It has joined its public advocacy with practical efforts to provide alternatives to abortion.

For all these reasons, I maintain that the witness to life in the past decade has been a cause for hope and pride. The lessons learned in the decade of the 1970's prepare us to analyze our choices in the 1980's.

The Present: Shaping Public Choices for Life

The effect of the pro-life movement has not been limited to its inspirational quality; there has been a specific political impact. Eleven years after the Supreme Court decisions and after a string of other legal actions reaffirming the *Roe v. Wade* philosophy, the pro-abortion philosophy has not been accepted by millions of Americans. In brief, the legal status of abortion still lacks public legitimacy. The political debate which ensued shows the nation radically divided on the state of public policy on abortion.

Normally, the force of existing law provides legitimacy for policy. Keeping the question open for reform and reversal of existing policy is a significant political victory. It is a tactical success. It should not, however, be mistaken for total success. Nonetheless, it provides space to move the nation toward a different future on abortion.

Creating space to change law and policy is a precondition for what must be accomplished. It is imperative in the 1980's to use the space creatively. In working to change national policy on abortion, I submit that we must cast our case in broadly defined terms in a way which elicits support from others. We need to shape our position consciously in a way designed to generate interest in the abortion question from individuals who thus far have not been touched by our witness or our arguments.

Casting our perspective broadly does not mean diluting its content. Quite the opposite. It involves a process of demonstrating how our position on abortion is deeply rooted in our religious tradition and, at the same time, is protective of fundamental ideas in our constitutional tradition.

Speaking from my perspective as a Roman Catholic bishop, I wish to affirm that the basis of our opposition to abortion is established by themes which should be compelling for the Catholic conscience because they are so centrally located in Catholic moral and social teaching. The basic moral principle that the direct killing of the innocent is always wrong is so fundamental in Catholic theology that the need to defend it in the multiple cases of abortion, warfare and care of the handicapped and the terminally ill is self-evident.

This is why one cannot, with consistency, claim to be truly pro-life if one applies the principle of the sanctity of life to other issues but rejects it in the case of abortion. By the same token, one cannot with consistency claim to be truly pro-life if one applies the principle to other issues, but holds that the direct targeting or killing of innocent non-combatants in warfare is morally justifiable. To fail to stand for this principle is to make a fundamental error in Catholic moral thought. But the moral principle does not stand alone; it is related to other dimensions of Catholic social teaching.

The opposition to abortion is rooted in the conviction that civil law and social policy must always be subject to ongoing moral analysis. Simply because a civil law is in place does not mean that it should be blindly supported. To encourage reflective, informed assessment of civil law and policy is to keep alive the capacity for moral criticism in society.

In addition, the Catholic position opposing abortion is rooted in our understanding of the role of the state in society. The state has positive moral responsibilites; it is not simply a neutral umpire; neither is its role limited to restraining evil. The responsibilities of the state include both the protection of innocent life from attack and enhancement of human life at every state of its development. The fact of 1.5 million abortions a year in the United States erodes the moral character of the state; if the civil law can be neutral when innocent life is under attack, the implications for law and morality in our society are truly frightening.

These themes drawn from Catholic theology are not restricted in their application to the community of faith. These are truths of the moral and political order which are also fundamental to the Western constitutional heritage. The opposition to abortion properly stated is not a sectarian claim, but a reflective, rational position which any person of good will may be invited to consider. Examples can be used to illustrate the convergence of our concerns about abortion with other key social questions in American society.

The appeal to a higher moral law to reform and refashion existing civil law was the central idea that Dr. Martin Luther King Jr. brought to the civil rights movement of the 1960's. The pro-life movement of the 1980's is based on the same appeal. Pro-life today should be seen as an extension of the spirit of the civil rights movement. In a similar way, the Baby Doe case has proved to be a meeting ground of principle and practice between civil rights and pro-life advocates. The common ground is as yet not sufficiently explored, but there is significant potential for development in this area.

Civil rights are the domestic application of the broader human rights tradition. The right to life is a fundamental basis of this tradition. By standing for the right to life in our society, we stand with all who argue for a strong national commitment to human rights in our domestic and foreign policy.

A final example of convergence is pertinent to your program today. Father Bruce Ritter has caught the imagination and interest of broad sectors of American society with his defense of human dignity in the face of sexual exploitation. The themes of the pro-life movement, promoting a sacred vision of sexuality and support for the family, coincide with Father Ritter's courageous and compassionate witness to life.

The Future: A Strategy for Witness to Life

It is precisely because I am convinced that demonstrating the linkage between abortion and other issues is both morally correct and tactically necessary for the pro-life position that I have been addressing the theme of a consistent ethic of life for church and society. The convergence of themes concerning civil rights, human rights and family life with the abortion issue is simply an indication of deeper bonds which exist along the full range of pro-life issues.

The proposals I have made on the linkage issues are, I submit, a systematic attempt to state the vision which has always been implicit in a Catholic conception of "pro-life." A Catholic view of the meaning of pro-life stresses the interdependence of life in a social setting, the way in which each of us relies upon the premise that others respect my life, and that society exists to guarantee that respect for each person. The interdependence of human life points toward the interrelationship of pro-life issues.

This interrelationship can be illustrated in precise, detailed moral arguments, but that is not the purpose of this address. I would simply appeal to a principle which I suspect is also an element of your own experience. It is the need to cultivate within society an attitude of respect for life on a series of issues, if the actions of individuals or groups are to reflect respect for life in specific choices.

The linkage theme of a consistent ethic of life is designed to highlight the common interest and reciprocal need which exist among groups interested in specific issues—peace, abortion, civil rights, justice for the dispossessed or disabled—each of which depends upon a basic attitude of respect for life. The linkage theme provides us with an opportunity to win "friends" for the life issues. Just as we insist on the principle of right to life, so too we must recognize the responsibility that our commitment places on us. Building bridges to people working on specific life issues demands respect and kindness toward these potential allies. An atmosphere of trust and understanding can do a great deal to promote the goals of the pro-life movement.

The consistent ethic seeks to build a bridge of common interest and common insight on a range of social and moral questions. It is designed to highlight the intrinsic ties which exist between public attitudes and personal actions on one side and public policy on the other. Effective defense of life requires a coordinated approach to attitude, action and policy. The consistent-ethic theme seeks to engage the moral imagination and political insight of diverse groups and to build a network of mutual concern for defense of life at every stage in the policies and practices of our society.

The need for such a common approach is dictated by the objective interrelationship among the life issues. The strength of the Catholic contribution to such an approach lies in the long and rich tradition of moral and social analysis which has provided us with both detailed guidance in individual moral issues and a framework for relating several issues in a coherent fashion.

If we pursue a consistent ethic systematically, it will become clear that abortion is not a "single issue" because it is not even a single kind of issue. It is an issue about the nature and future of the family, both in its own right and as a basic unit of society. It is an issue about equality under law for all human beings. It is an issue of life or death. For this reason, developments in all these areas may not always be the direct responsibility of each person in the right-to-life movement, but they should always be of intense interest to all.

Whatever makes our society more human, more loving, more respectful of the life and dignity of others, is a contribution to your struggle; for the more committed society becomes to justice and compassion, the more incongruous will be its toleration of the killing of the unborn child. And whatever promotes respect for that child cannot help but promote respect for all humanity. With that in mind, I urge you to recommit yourselves with renewed energy to this great cause. Where humanity is threatened at its most defenseless, we have no choice. We must stand up on its behalf.

(Origins, July 12, 1984. Vol. 14: No. 8.)

Bibliography and Supplemental Resources

The following is a list of resources that can be used to supplement the text. These resources go beyond our life issues of abortion, euthanasia and suicide. They include a whole range of bio-medical ethical materials. This list of resources is also part of a cassette program offered by ALBA HOUSE COMMUNICATIONS in Canfield, Ohio.

Journals

Bioethics Quarterly (Northwest Institute of Ethics and the Life Sciences, 6241 31st Ave., N.E., Seattle, Washington 98115).

The Hasting Center Report (360 Broadway, Hastings-on-Hudson, NY 10706).

Journal of Medicine and Philosophy (Society for Health and Human Values, 925 Chestnut St., Philadelphia, PA 19107).

Linacre Quarterly (National Federation of Catholic Physicians' Guilds, 8430 W. Capitol Drive, Milwaukee, WS 53222).

American Journal of Law and Medicine.

American Journal of Medicine.

American Journal of Psychiatry.

Ethics.

Journal of the American Medical Association.

New England Journal of Medicine.

Film Resources

Projection 70's Medicine. Color. 16mm. 25 minutes. Rent: $25.00. Distributor: American Educational Films, 132 Lasky Drive, Beverly Hills, CA 90212.

Abortion and the Law. Black and White. 16mm. 54 minutes. No charge. Distributor: Cuyahoga County Public Library, 4510 Memphis Avenue, Cleveland, OH.

Conversations in Medical Ethics: Abortion. Black and White. 16mm. 10 minutes. Rent: Free to Physicians. Distributor: Student American Medical Association, 2635 Flossmoor Road, Flossmoor, IL 60422.

Intra-Uterine Diagnosis in Early Pregnancy: Fetal, Parental and Societal Considerations. Black and White. ¾" Video Cassette. 60 minutes. Sale: $68.00. Distributor: Dr. Bernard Towers, Department of Pediatrics, School of Medicine, U.C.L.A., Los Angeles, CA 90024.

Death. Black and White. 16mm. Rent: $35.00. Sale: $275.00. Distributor: Filmmakers Library, Inc., 290 West End Avenue, New York, NY 10020.

To Die Today. Black and White. 16mm. 50 minutes. Rent: $35.00. Sale: $275.00. Distributor: Filmmakers Library, Inc., 290 West End Avenue, New York, NY 10020.

Must We Redefine Death? Black and White. ¾" Video Cassette. 60 minutes. Sale: $68.00. Distributor: Dr. Bernard Towers, Department of Pediatrics, School of Medicine, U.C.L.A., Los Angeles, CA 90024.

Please Let Me Die. Color. Video Tape. 30 minutes. Rent $25.00. Sale: $100.00. Distributor: Library of Clinical Psychiatric Syndromes, Dr. Robert B. White, Department of Psychiatry, University of Texas Medical Branch, Galveston TX 77550.

The Right to Die. Color. 50 mm. 60 minutes. Rent: $55.00. Sale: $600.00. Distributor: Macmillan, Vernon, NY 10660.

Who Should Survive? Color. 16mm. 26 minutes. Rent: $20.00. Sale: $150.00. Distributor: Patricia Furman, 209 East Broad Street, Falls Church, Virginia 22046.

Gifts of Life/Right to Die. Black and White. 16mm. 16 minutes. Rent: $4.40. Distributor: Visual Aids Service. Division of University Extension, University of Illinois, Champaign, IL 61822.

Ethical Problems in Medical Research. Color, Video Tape. 26 minutes. Distributor: University of Texas Medical School at San Antonio, Department of Medical Communications Research, San Antonio, TX.

For the Safety of Mankind. Color. 16mm. 26 minutes. Rent: $30.00. Sale: $275.00. Distributor: Time-Life Films, 45 West 16th Street, New York, NY 10011.

Organizations

Committee for Philosophy and Medicine (American Philosophical Association: Headquarters at University of Delaware, Neward, Delaware 19711).

The Hastings Center, Institute for Society, Ethics, and the Life Sciences (360 Broadway, Hastings-on-Hudson, NY 10706).

The Joseph and Rose Kennedy Institute of Ethics (Georgetown University, Washington, D.C. 20057).

Ministers in Medical Education (Sixth Floor, 925 Chestnut Street, Philadelphia, PA 19107).

The Society for Health and Human Values (Sixth Floor, 925 Chestnut Street, Philadelphia, PA 19107).

Introductory Materials

Beauchamp, Tom L. and Childress, James F., *Principles of Biomedical Ethics.* New York: Oxford University Press, 1979.

D'Arsy, Eric, *Conscience and Its Right to Freedom.* New York: Sheed and Ward, 1961.

Dedek, John F., *Contemporary Medical Ethics.* New York: Sheed and Ward, 1975.

Haring, Bernard, *Medical Ethics.* Notre Dame, IN: Fides Publishers, 1973.

Ramsey, Paul, *Deeds and Rules in Christian Ethics.* New York: Charles Scribner's Sons, 1967.

Reich, Warren T. ed., *Encyclopedia of Bioethics.* Four volumes. New York: The Free Press, 1978.

Shannon, Thomas A., ed., *Bioethics.* New York: Paulist Press, 1976 and a new revised edition in 1981.

Varga, Andrew C., *The Main Issues in Bioethics.* New York: Paulist Press, 1980.

Veatch, Robert M., *Case Studies in Medical Ethics*. Cambridge: Harvard University Press, 1977.

Abortion

Callahan, Daniel, *Abortion: Law, Choice and Morality*. New York: Macmillan, 1970.

Grisez, Germain, *Abortion: The Myth, the Realities and the Arguments*. New York: World Publishing Company, Inc., 1981.

McCormick, Richard A., *How Brave a New World? Dilemmas in Bioethics*. New York: Doubleday and Company, Inc., 1981.

Noonan, John T., Jr., *A Private Choice: Abortion in America in the Seventies*. New York: The Free Press, 1979.

Ramsey, Paul, *Ethics at the Edge of Life: Medical and Legal Intersections*. New Haven: Yale University Press, 1978.

Behavior Control

Delgado, Jose M.R., *Physical Control of the Mind: Toward a Psycho-Civilized Society*. New York: Harper and Row, 1969.

Gaylin, William M., Meister, Joe S., and Neville, Robert C., editors, *Operating on Mind*. New York: Basic Books, 1975.

London, Perry, *Behavior Control*. New York: The New American Library, 1977.

Skinner, B.F., *Beyond Freedom and Dignity*. New York: Alfred A. Knopf, 1971.

Silverman, Milton and Lee, Philip R., *Pills, Profits and Politics*. Berkeley: University of California Press, 1974.

Death and Dying

Aries, Philippe, *Western Attitudes Toward Death: From the Middle Ages to the Present*. Trans. by Patricia M. Ranum. Baltimore: John Hopkins University Press, 1974.

Becher, Ernest, *The Denial of Death*. New York: The Free Press, 1973.

Bok, Sissela, *Dying: Moral Choices in Public and Private Life*. New York: Pantheon Books, 1978.

Boros, Ladislaus, *The Mystery of Death*. New York: Herder and Herder, 1965.

Kohl, Marvin, ed., *Beneficient Euthanasia*. Buffalo: Prometheus Books, 1975.
Kubler-Ross, Elizabeth, *On Death and Dying*. New York, Macmillan Press, 1969.
Maguire, Daniel C., *Death by Choice*. New York: Doubleday, 1974.
Veatch, Robert M., *Death, Dying and the Biological Revolution*. New Haven: Yale University Press, 1976.
Weber, Leonard J., *Who Shall Live? The Dilemma of Severely Handicapped Children and its Meaning for Other Moral Questions*. New York: Paulist Press, 1976.

Genetic Engineering

Etzioni, Amitai, *Genetic Fix: The Next Technological Revolution*. New York: Harper and Row, 1973.
Francoeur, Robert T., *Utopian Motherhood*. New York: Doubleday, 1970.
Kass, Leon R., "Babies by Means of *In Vitro* Fertilization: Unethical Experiments on the Unborn?" *New England Journal of Medicine*. 285 (November 18, 1971), 1174-1179.
Lappe, Mare, ed., *Ethical and Scientific Issues Posed by Human Uses of Molecular Genetics*. New York: The New York Academy of Sciences, 1976.
Ramsey, Paul, *Fabricated Man: The Ethics of Genetic Control*. New Haven: Yale University Press, 1970.
Wade, Nicholas, *The Ultimate Experiment*. New York: Walker and Company, 1977.

Human Experimentation

Annas, George J., Glarz, Leonard H., and Katz, Barbara F., *Informed Consent to Human Experimentation: The Subject's Dilemma*. Cambridge, Mass.: The Ballinger Publishing Co., 1977.
Beecher, Henry K., *Research and the Individual: Human Studies*. Boston: Little, Brown and Company, 1970.
Cowles, Jane, *Informed Consent*. New York: Coward, McCann and Geoghegan, 1976.

Levy, Charlotte L., *The Human Body and the Law: Legal and Ethical Considerations in Human Experimentation*. Dobbs Ferry, New York, Oceana Publications, 1975.

Ramsey, Paul, *The Ethics of Fetal Research*. New Haven: Yale University Press, 1975.

Visscher, Maurice B., *Ethical Constraints and Imperatives in Medical Research*. Springfield, IL, Charles C. Thomas, Publisher, 1975.

Newborns/Birth Defects

Duff, Raymond S., and Campbell, A.G.M., "Moral and Ethical Dilemmas in the Special-Care Nursery," *New England Journal of Medicine* 289 (October 25, 1973), 890-894.

Fletcher, John C., "Abortion, Euthanasia and Care of Defective Newborns," *New England Journal of Medicine* 292 (January 9, 1975), 75-78.

Gustafson, James M., "Mongolism, Parental Desires and the Right to Life," *Perspectives in Biology and Medicine* 16 (Summer 1973), 529-557.

Ludmerer, Kenneth M., *Genetics and American Society: A Historical Appraisal*. Baltimore: Johns Hopkins University Press, 1972.

Stevenson, Alan C. et al., *Genetic Counseling*. Philadelphia: J.B. Lippincott Co., 1977.

Organ Transplantation

Lyons, Catherine, *Organ Transplants: The Moral Issues*. Philadelphia: The Westminster Press, 1970.

Miller, George W., *Moral and Ethical Implications of Human Organ Transplants*. Springfield, IL. Charles C. Thomas, Publisher, 1971.

Schmeck, Harold M., Jr., *The Semi-Artificial Man: A Dawning Revolution in Medicine*. New York: Walker and Company, 1965.

Patient Rights

Belski, Marvin S., and Gross, Leonard, *How to Choose and Use Your Doctor*. New York: Arbor House Publishing Company, 1975.

Cassell, Eric J., *The Healer's Art: A New Approach to the Doctor-Patient Relationship*. Philadelphia: J.B. Lippincott Company, 1976.

Illich, Ivan, *Medical Nemesis*. New York: Pantheon Books, 1976.

Krause, Elliot A., *Power and Illness*. New York: Elsevier, 1977.

Lewis, Charles E., et al., *A Right to Health—The Problem of Access to Medical Care*. New York: John Wiley and Sons, 1976.